PROPHETS
IN THEIR OWN COUNTRY

PROPHETS
IN THEIR OWN COUNTRY

*Women Religious Bearing Witness to the Gospel
in a Troubled Church*

SANDRA M. SCHNEIDERS, IHM

ORBIS BOOKS
Maryknoll, New York 10545

Founded in 1970, Orbis Books endeavors to publish works that enlighten the mind, nourish the spirit, and challenge the conscience. The publishing arm of the Maryknoll Fathers and Brothers, Orbis seeks to explore the global dimensions of the Christian faith and mission, to invite dialogue with diverse cultures and religious traditions, and to serve the cause of reconciliation and peace. The books published reflect the views of their authors and do not represent the official position of the Maryknoll Society. To learn more about Maryknoll and Orbis Books, please visit our website at www.maryknollsociety.org.

Library of Congress Cataloging-in-Publication Data

Schneiders, Sandra Marie.
  Prophets in their own country : women religious bearing witness to the Gospel in a troubled church / Sandra M. Schneiders.
    p. cm.
  ISBN 978-1-57075-933-8
  1. Monastic and religious life of women—United States. 2. Visitations, Ecclesiastical—United States. 3. Catholic Church—United States. I. Title.
  BX4220.U6S36 2011
  271'.900973—dc22
                                    2011000689

In gratitude
to women Religious worldwide
and
to the many thousands of Catholic lay people in the United States
for your confidence in, support for, and solidarity with
American women Religious

CONTENTS

ACKNOWLEDGMENTS

Although I am fully responsible for the contents of this book, I am deeply conscious of the people without whose help it could not have been written. I am especially grateful to Tom Fox, publisher and editor of the *National Catholic Reporter*, who originally invited, indeed urged, me to publish something about the Apostolic Visitation and subsequently solicited or accepted the pieces which followed and which appear in this book. Over the years Tom has been a staunch and effective supporter of women Religious whose lives and ministry, and whose struggles in society and Church, he deeply appreciates. Without his initiative I would probably not have written anything about the Visitation and certainly not a collection of essays.

Robert Ellsberg, publisher of Orbis Books, who has acted as editor for this volume, was immediately interested in responding to the request of many people to get the *NCR* material out in a more permanent form, and I am grateful for his help in doing so. Tom and Robert represent surely the best in Catholic publishing and I—with so many others—am deeply in their debt.

My own congregation, the Sisters, Servants of the Immaculate Heart of Mary of Monroe, Michigan, in the persons of our leadership council and especially Sister Carol Quigley, IHM, have been totally supportive of my efforts and of me personally. I am well aware how fortunate I am to belong to a prophetic community willing to take risks for the sake of the Gospel.

ix

I also want to thank Sister Jane Burke, SSND, and Sister Annmarie Sanders, IHM, from the office of the Leadership Conference of Women Religious who generously read parts of this material and prevented me from making some potentially serious errors of fact. They have not, I am sure, been able to prevent all errors of judgment but for the latter I am solely responsible.

My gratitude also to my research assistant, Ms. Jen Owens, who went beyond the call of duty in carefully proofreading the entire manuscript within a very tight time frame.

Finally, and by no means least, I want to thank the thousands of women Religious in the United States, Canada, and Australia with whom I have shared this material over the past two years and who have responded so enthusiastically to my efforts. I have been strengthened by their sharing of their own experience and reflection. The mutual affirmation, solidarity, and commitment we have experienced during this time has supported all of us, but especially me, in the effort to articulate our identity and mission as women Religious in our deeply troubled Church.

INTRODUCTION

The Relation of This Book to Its Historical Context

This is a book I never intended to write. It began as a series of articles that were published in the *National Catholic Reporter* (*NCR*) between February 2009 and January 2010 occasioned by the "Apostolic Visitation of Institutes of Women Religious in the United States" that was launched by the Vatican in January 2009 and is scheduled for completion by "confidential reports" on the Institutes to the Vatican in 2011—after this book has gone to press. Although "apostolic visitation" is the canonical term for this process, it is more widely referred to by those undergoing it or observing it as the "Vatican investigation" of U.S. women Religious. Because this latter term describes more accurately what is actually going on, it is the term I use most often in these essays.

All books, in one way or another, emerge from their own historical context, but this one has a unique relationship to the current situation of American Religious Life. The book is not intended even as a chronicle, much less a history, of the Vatican investigation or the response of U.S. Religious to it. I leave that to historians who are better equipped than I to sift through the documents, discern causes and effects, and evaluate outcomes. When that history is written it will undoubtedly make available the original texts and documents, material on the principal actors in the drama, and

1

eventual results generated by the investigation itself, but this is not my project. However, since each piece—letter, article, or essay—that has become a chapter of this book was occasioned by some aspect of the investigation, it would be difficult to understand the individual chapters or their relationship to the overall project without situating them, at least briefly, in the context of that experience. My purpose in writing the original pieces was to reflect on the nature of apostolic or ministerial Religious Life as it is being developed and lived by women Religious in the United States (and, of course, elsewhere with cultural variations that are important but not pertinent to this particular project). Publishing these originally separate pieces together as a book is a response to repeated requests by individuals, groups, and congregations to make all the material available in a concise and manageable format. So, with the generous permission of the *NCR* and the cooperation of Orbis Books I am offering them, with minimal editing, for the use of Religious and laity who have an interest in the subject.

In this introduction I want to supply the historical, sociological, and ecclesiological context to help readers, Catholic and non-Catholic, Religious and laity, especially people unfamiliar with the workings of the Vatican bureaucracy (the Roman Curia), to understand the individual chapters. The global context is the Vatican investigation and the reaction to it on the part of Religious themselves as well as others. The Vatican, by the way it initiated the investigation, clearly intended not only to take the Religious congregations completely by surprise and thus seize the tactical advantage in the juridical process, but also to keep the process ecclesiastically "in house"—presenting it as a simple and straightforward case of the highest Church authority legitimately investigating some of its subordinates.

Religious were indeed "blindsided" by the announcement of the investigation at a public press conference in

Washington, DC, without any consultation of the Religious who were its target, and with only a fax and phone call an hour before the press conference to the national office of the Leadership Conference of Women Religious (LCWR) alerting them to the imminent announcement. Even major superiors themselves were not accorded the courtesy of an informational letter before the fact. Nevertheless, Religious organized themselves within weeks before the Vatican could capitalize on the element of surprise and the whole affair exploded into the public's consciousness in and outside the Church within days of its initiation. It was another example, like the clergy pedophile scandal and the episcopal facilitation of it and obstruction of justice once it became public, of how current electronic communication media make the once viable "confidential" (read: secret or clandestine) inner workings of the higher echelons of the ecclesiastical power structure unworkable. Not only did the secular media, such as the *New York Times*, National Public Radio, and the national television networks, immediately pick up and begin independent investigations of the story, but Catholic laity all over the country and outside it, and Religious from many parts of the world began to ask probing questions about what was going on and to weigh in with their own opinions on the subject, including speculation on possible nefarious Vatican motivations. The Vatican investigation of U.S. women Religious became a *cause célèbre* almost overnight.

My involvement, which I probably would never have initiated on my own since I am not in a leadership position in my own congregation nor at the national level, arose "by accident" when a Sister e-mailed me and a few of our theological colleagues to express her shock and alarm at the launching of the investigation. Where did this bolt from the blue come from? Why was it happening? What did it portend? How could/should/must we respond?

I had been aware that a "Symposium on Apostolic Religious Life since Vatican II" had been held a couple of months earlier at Stonehill College near Boston ostensibly to celebrate the 200th anniversary of the archdiocese. At the time I suspected, given what I had heard about speakers and topics, that it had some connection, official or unofficial, with the small but organized contingent of American women Religious who have found the conciliar renewal of Religious Life very distressing. Whatever the actual connection, virtually all the speakers at the symposium turned out to be connected to, representative of, or in sympathy with the views of this group whose public face is the Conference of Major Superiors of Women Religious (CMSWR).

CMSWR obtained Vatican approval in 1995 to function as a kind of conservative alternative (or even "competition") to the Leadership Conference of Women Religious (LCWR), which includes the leadership of the vast majority (90 percent or more) of American congregations and was, until 1995, the sole official representative of American women Religious to the Vatican (parallel to the Conference of Major Superiors of Men [CMSM]). LCWR (originally called the Conference of Major Superiors of Women [CMSW]) was initiated at the request of Pius XII in the 1950s. The CMSWR (not related to CMSW, CMSM, or LCWR) is the successor of the Consortium Perfectae Caritatis [CPC], a very small group of superiors who broke away from LCWR in 1971 because they believed LCWR-type Religious congregations were unfaithful to the "essential elements" of Religious Life— a suspicion that subsequently was officially laid to rest, it was thought, in the early 1980s when the "Quinn Commission" appointed by John Paul II to investigate U.S. women Religious reassured the Vatican that American Religious Life was not in disarray.

At the time of that earlier "evaluation," the Vatican bureau that oversees Religious Life (then called the Sacred

Congregation for Religious and Secular Institutes or SCRSI, which was the precursor of the present Congregation for Institutes of Consecrated Life and Societies of Apostolic Life or CICLSAL) had produced a document intended as a "guide" for that investigation. The document was eventually known by its abbreviated title, "Essential Elements of Religious Life." It was a regressive and repressive document that was basically stillborn. It was never promulgated because its formulators had been unable to garner even the requisite number of signatures from Vatican officials themselves to obtain papal approval or recognition of its contents, and it was never accepted by the vast majority of Religious themselves. Thus, unpromulgated and unreceived, the document was otiose from its inception, and the Vatican wisely allowed it to "disappear" from the scene although it is still "on the books" as issuing "from the Vatican" (not from SCRSI or by permission of the Pope). However, a small minority of Religious congregations, or at least their leadership, made that document a kind of "magna carta" for their own understanding of conciliar renewal, and this minority considers itself the faithful remnant defending authentic Religious Life as expressed in "Essential Elements" from the vast majority of their Sisters who, in their opinion, have gone astray.

Although LCWR freely welcomes without preconditions the participation of CMSWR superiors in its organization and at its meetings, this welcome is not reciprocated and a kind of one-way polarization has been created between the two organizations—the traditionalist group defining itself over against LCWR, which, while not sharing some of the CMSWR's convictions, has always recognized that a variety of approaches to the life is possible and legitimate and that differences in such matters need not and should not lead to animosity or rejection.

Whether or not CMSWR was officially involved in its organization, the symposium on Religious Life that took place

at Stonehill College on September 27, 2008, was basically a
rallying event for this traditionalist minority group. At the
time I somewhat naïvely considered the event relatively in-
nocuous. Such was not the case. The organizers had invited
to the symposium Cardinal Franc Rodé, prefect (that is, the
head) of CICLSAL, the current Vatican bureau that deals
with matters pertaining to Religious congregations. The Cardinal is well known for his conviction that Vatican II precipitated the first worldwide crisis in the Church's history and
for his deep apprehensions about American Religious, particularly women, whom he thinks are "in crisis" due to their
surrender to "secularist" and "feminist" trends, both negative epithets in his vocabulary.

Among the speakers at the symposium was a lay journal-
ist, Ann Carey, a self-appointed expert on Religious Life
(which she has never lived) who, for years, has been a vocal
and often vitriolic critic lamenting what she calls "the tragic
unraveling" (that is, the conciliar renewal) of Religious Life.
Perhaps the most important speaker at the symposium, however, was Sister Sara Butler, SMBT, a theologian renowned
for her forceful and public opposition to women's ordination and to the developments in mainstream American Religious Life since the Council, the first of which she believes is
unfaithful to Church teaching and the second scandalous to
the Catholic faithful.

In her symposium address Sister Butler explicitly called
on the cardinal to initiate an "apostolic visitation" of American women Religious. Many Religious, used to the kind of
openness and solidarity characteristic of the American sister-
hood, considered this public call of one Religious for official
hierarchical investigation of her peers shocking. But I, however, did not believe such a singular plea would be taken seriously in high places, at least not without extensive consultation with a much broader spectrum of more representative
voices. Nevertheless, as soon became clear, Sister Butler was

voicing the cardinal's own deepest anxieties, and within three months Rodé did exactly what Butler had urged. We will undoubtedly never know if there was a causal connection between these two facts (although Rodé alluded to the Symposium in replying to questions about his decision to investigate U.S. women Religious), but the peculiar shape and very untraditional character of the investigation suggests that, wherever it came from, it was a hasty and ill-conceived initiative at best.

I responded, no doubt with a naïve hope that cooler ecclesiastical heads would prevail, to the e-mail sent to me by my colleague by suggesting that the whole matter did not warrant such alarm and the less attention paid to it the better. However, in that e-mail, which turned out to be a kind of "shot heard round the Religious world" and which constitutes chapter 1 of this book, I did devote some time to analyzing the increasing tension between the CMSWR and the LCWR visions of Vatican II, the renewal of Religious Life called for by the Council and undertaken by the vast majority of women Religious (even while being resisted by a small minority), and the probable relation of that tension between U. S. Religious to the investigation. It was in that e-mail that I stated unambiguously what has become the leitmotif of the material in this book, namely, my conviction that post-conciliar women Religious have given birth, finally, to a new form of Religious Life (not of consecrated life, which is a different matter altogether) that has been struggling into existence for some four hundred years and that I was calling "ministerial Religious Life."

As the preamble to chapter 1 explains, it was not my intention that that e-mail ever become public. (I also had much to learn about the non-controllability of electronic media!). But in fact, without anyone's malicious intentions, it circulated rapidly and widely, and a large number of people inside and outside Religious Life, in the ranks and in leadership, found it helpful. They asked the editor of the *NCR*, Tom Fox, a great friend of Religious, to publish the e-mail and he prevailed upon me to allow that. Because the piece had already been so widely circulated, and some people had begun to make friendly "editorial" modifications to the text for the sake of clarity for those with whom they shared it, it seemed a good idea to establish a "canonical text" with which people could agree or disagree but which was at least accurate. The publication of that brief text thrust me into the public furor that the investigation had already generated and what followed is the tumultuous history women Religious have been living for the past two years.

Chapter 2 of this book is an essay written shortly thereafter explictly for the *NCR* in which I tried to answer the two questions about the investigation that seemed to be on everyone's mind, "Why is this investigation taking place? And why are Religious so incensed about it?" To respond to those questions I had to explain what an "apostolic visitation" is, that is, why it is not comparable to a routine evaluation like an accreditation visit to a school or any other kind of in-house ordinary evaluation of subordinates by legitimate superiors. An apostolic visitation is a juridical process imposed on (and occasionally requested by) an ecclesiastical unit (diocese, order, institution, etc.) which is credibly accused or suspected of or embroiled in serious moral, religious, spiritual, doctrinal, financial, civil, or other types of misconduct or conflict whose solution the unit in question cannot, or will not, undertake on its own.

Rarely in history have entire Religious orders (much less all the Religious in a country) been subjected to such processes (see Church historian Gary Macy's article on the subject in the July 6, 2009, issue of the *NCR*). Perhaps the clearest example of a legitimate apostolic visitation of a Religious order of pontifical right (that is, one that transcends diocesan jurisdiction) is the recently completed visitation of the Legionnaires of Christ whose founder was patently guilty of massive, decades-long sexual and financial violations and who had created such an internal system of secrecy, spying, and manipulation and such an external system of high-level corruption and collusion that he was virtually untouchable. He was at the center of a vast international network of scandal and had a moral stranglehold on thousands of young Religious within his congregation, several of whom he had been sexually abusing for years, who had been brainwashed into blind adulation and intimidated into blind submission. The apostolic visitation of the Legionnaires was absolutely necessary to stop an otherwise unstoppable tidal wave of grave scandal and abuse.

The nature of an apostolic visitation with its implied accusation and presumed guilt (despite disingenuous assurances that such are not intended in the present case) was galling to women Religious, most of whom have lived in their communities for four, five, six or more decades, faithful to their vows and constitutions and in full-time service of God's people. Their distress was exacerbated by the blatant discrimination involved in the selection of women's (but not men's) apostolic (but not enclosed) orders, U.S. "units" (but not the communities, provinces, or even motherhouses of those same orders that are located outside U.S. borders but are governed by the same constitutions, chapter enactments, traditions, superiors as those in the United States). But the methods being used in the investigation were perhaps the most objectionable aspect of the process. They were so lacking in transparency, mutuality, respect, and even honesty that they could be regarded by most Americans only as totalitarian if not fascist. They made the entire process appear to most Sisters as hypocritical and even violent.

Although these reasons easily answered the second question—Why are Religious upset, even incensed, about the investigation?—it proved impossible then, and it remains impossible now, to extract any clear answer to the first question—Why are Religious being investigated? No credible answer to that question was forthcoming from Cardinal Rodé, CICLSAL, or the sole official "visitator" of some four hundred groups including close to sixty thousand members, Mary Clare Millea, ASCJ. Neither "quality of life" (unless that quality is sinful or depraved in some way) nor "declining numbers of entrants" (unless, perhaps, that is due to some evil for which the Religious are responsible) are sins, crimes, or even disorders. All mollifying rhetoric to the contrary notwithstanding, everyone knew very well that apostolic visitations are not undertaken to showcase the virtues of the accused any more than a grand jury is convened to lift up the sterling quality of life of the defendant.

Because there was no intelligible content to the "quality of life" charge I turned my attention to the question of numbers. But rather than ask why so few new candidates were entering Religious Life—the answer to which was simple enough and had nothing to do with the laxity or turpitude of the current members—I asked why such a huge number of young women entered at the time of the "surge" in the 1950s and 1960s, and even more significantly why some sixty thousand have stayed despite the powerful incentives to leave to which large numbers of their companions responded in the immediate post-conciliar period. Those incentives were numerous and varied but certainly included the pressure of disapproval and even persecution by the official Church. It was that analysis that led the *NCR* to entitle the article "Why They Stay(ed)."

The article struck a very deep chord in the consciousness of many Religious who found that it resonated strongly with their experience and affirmed their most profoundly held and long-practiced commitments. The response to this article made clear to me that there was a widespread hunger for some clear and accessible biblical and theological material on the history, nature, conciliar renewal, and spirituality of contemporary ministerial Religious Life that could serve as context for dealing not only with the immediate problem of the investigation but also, and more important, for reflecting on our life, discussing it among ourselves, and communicating about it to interested supporters or critics.

For Religious the need was primarily for *articulation*, for putting words on their rapidly changing experience of the life which most had been too busy living, especially through the post-conciliar renewal period, to have had time to describe in detail for themselves or their families, friends, and colleagues. Many non-Religious needed some clearer *understanding* of the "changes" they had observed in Religious Life over the past few decades. As became abundantly clear in the widespread vigorous defense of Religious by the laity in the months after the investigation was launched, the mainstream Catholic laity have not been "scandalized" or "demoralized" by the life and ministry of Religious (as they certainly have been by that of some of the clergy and hierarchy). Indeed, they are deeply appreciative and supportive of their Sisters who themselves have become much closer to their lay friends and co-ministers since the Council. But these lay supporters were now seeking a better understanding of the sources and meaning of the sometimes quiet, sometimes dramatic, changes in Religious Life over the past few decades. Since I have spent the last ten years engaged in research, consultation, and writing about ministerial Religious Life I felt some responsibility, even in advance of the publication of the third volume of my trilogy *Religious Life in a New Millennium*, to make some of this work available immediately to a wider public.

I tried to respond to this urgent need for concise, clear articulation of "what was going on" in Religious Life in what is now chapter 3 of this volume, "Discerning Ministerial Religious Life Today," which came out in the *NCR* in September

2009 under the title "The Past and Future of Ministerial Religious Life." The chapter has two parts that are crucial to an understanding of the current situation. The first is a brief but I hope adequate overview of the *historical development of non-cloistered Religious Life from Trent to Vatican II,* that is, of the immediate *past* of what I have begun calling "ministerial Religious Life." I chose this "new" designation to distinguish the current form of women's Religious Life from the hybrid apostolic/monastic form that had developed in the period from the 1500s when non-cloistered Religious Life for women began to find some quasi-official acceptance in the Church up to Vatican Council II.

This form of the life, which is that of the vast majority of women Religious today, is usually called "apostolic Religious Life," although its proper juridical title under which it was canonically recognized in 1900 was "Congregations Devoted to Works of the Apostolate." The latter title captures precisely the problem, or at least the ambiguity, of the term "apostolic Religious Life," namely, that ministry in such congregations continued, during this long period of development, to be regarded as a *"secondary end,"* an "overflow" activity, even an (often distracting) "appendage" as it were, to the substance of the life, which was still seen as essentially and ideally at least semi-cloistered and monastic. Furthermore, like the "apostolates of the laity," which began to be recognized in roughly the same historical period, the "apostolates of Religious" tended to be seen as "good works" (apostolates) *delegated* to them by the clergy or hierarchy who alone were called to ministry, rather than as a constitutive dimension of their life as Religious, rooted in the charism of the lifeform itself, which is intrinsically and pervasively ministerial regardless of what types of apostolates or "works" the Religious undertake.

The second part of the article, then, is a biblical-theological description and analysis of the essentially *ministerial* nature of contemporary Religious Life (its *present and future*) as it has come to be understood and lived among non-cloistered Religious. I attempted to demonstrate the validity and importance of this "new" (although actually several centuries in the making) form of Religious Life that finally "emerged" fully, as clearly distinct from enclosed monastic life, in the wake of the Council.

The crux of this part of the essay was to identify the roots of the new consciousness, and the resulting new lifeform, of women Religious. The contemporary development of this form of Religious Life is deeply rooted in the Council's radical challenge to the whole Church—especially in the documents on the Church (*Lumen Gentium*) and the Church in the Modern World (*Gaudium et Spes*)—to abandon its world-denying Tridentine defensiveness and wholeheartedly espouse Jesus' mission to extend to the "world which God so loved" the universal salvific love of God. This embrace of "mission to the world" had led, in the aftermath of the Council, to a putting aside of such characteristics of monastic life as conspicuous uniform dress (habits), enclosed housing (cloister), and daily identical schedules of group prayer, meals, recreation, and so forth (horarium). These features, ministerial Religious claimed, were not "essential elements" of Religious Life itself but of one historical form of the life, namely, monasticism.

Once again, the response to the article from women Religious was overwhelmingly positive. For me, the best test of the validity of anything I write about Religious Life is whether the people who have been living the life over decades recognize in my articulation their own lived experience and find in it affirmation and encouragement to continue. In other words, the living of the life precedes and must validate any theoretical treatment of it, whether such treatment comes from Church officials or theologians. In the weeks after the article appeared it also received a very welcome professional endorsement from Notre Dame University theologian Richard McBrien. He urged people, especially some ill-informed (mostly lay male) "bloggers" who were pontificating on the true meaning and essential requirements of women's Religious Life and the absolute need for Vatican intervention to "rein in" these unfaithful women, to read the article before continuing their crusade for "orthodoxy" and "pure morals." He also provided a handy summary of the highlights of the article for the "general interest" public.

The final installment of the *NCR* series was a long article entitled "Religious Life as a Prophetic Lifeform," which the editors of the *NCR* strategically decided to publish in five sections appearing daily between January 4 and 8, 2010. These five installments constitute the final chapter of this book. This chapter was precipitated by the ongoing development of the process of the investigation, which became ever more disturbing. I sensed that a much deeper question was being raised by these increasingly repressive developments. It had to do with why the living of their vocation—which Religious have never claimed was perfect but which has been, by any measure, basically faithful and generous (because very few competent people would continue in this life today for any reason other than fidelity to a genuine vocation to it)—has precipitated such a profoundly negative reaction from Church authority. To get to that question, which is deeply disturbing if not truly agonizing for Religious, it is important to realize how the investigation has progressively revealed its true nature.

Phase One had required the highest superiors of all "units" under investigation to communicate in person or in writing a self-description of their community to the visitator, Sister Millea. Most superiors apparently did something to fulfill this rather vague requirement, taking advantage of it, in many cases, to make clear that their communities were internally quite healthy and stable but that their most serious problems were externally generated, to some extent by the culture and especially the economy, but most notably by the institutional Church: misogyny and discrimination against women, unavailability of sacramental nourishment, clericalism operative especially in ministry situations, hierarchical and clerical scandal which undermine confidence in the Church and its ministers, inadequate compensation and poor personnel policies and practices in many dioceses where Sisters ministered, official disrespect and suspicion of which the investigation itself was a prime example, etc. Even the visitator seemed to have been impressed with the confidence, indeed pride, in their communities evinced by the leaders. And some of the latter began to hope that perhaps the investigation could be turned in a positive direction, a kind of appreciative exposé and positive recognition of what post-conciliar Religious Life had become. This hope was bolstered by the simultaneous opening of the extraordinary traveling museum exhibition, "Women & Spirit," mounted by the LCWR to present the history and constitutive role of women Religious in the founding and building of the U.S. Catholic Church. This hope was, if not naïve, at least short-lived.

Phase Two began badly by the imposition on the congregations of a massive, detailed, and highly intrusive questionnaire clearly designed to elicit not relevant or useful information for the congregations' improvement but self incriminating evidence of laxity and secularism, disobedience to Church law and teaching, disloyalty to the hierarchy, and, of course, the hated "feminism," as well as infidelity to the obligations of Religious Life itself. It also sought to extract personnel and financial information that would set congregations up for internal manipulation and disciplinary repression if not expropriation of their "patrimony" (assets), which major superiors are charged to protect. The widespread polite but resolute refusal of leaders to supply the latter set of data led to the withdrawal of the questions, which required confidential personal information about Sisters (information that even civil law protects) and internal financial data about the congregation.

While a few congregations chose to respond in detail to the remaining parts of the questionnaire many, after careful consultation with canon lawyers, with one another, and with their membership, decided to reply to only some of the questions and/or to respond with extreme reserve, qualitatively and quantitatively. And some congregations simply submitted their approved constitutions as an adequate and accurate response to the questions and evidence of fidelity to their obligations. The clear message delivered in various ways was, "This is what we have committed ourselves to; this is what the official Church has approved; this is what we are living."

The apostolic visitation office, apparently reflecting Cardinal Rodé's displeasure at this respectful but clear exercise of self-determination, "invited" those congregations that had not supplied detailed responses to all of the questions to re-do their questionnaires, a request to which, apparently, few if any congregations responded.

Meanwhile the cardinal had asked the American bishops to assume the $1.1 million cost of the investigation (a greater expenditure than the Vatican had undertaken for all the material preparations for the Second Vatican Council!) and, not receiving a positive response, then appealed to individual U.S. bishops to "contribute" to defraying the cost. Few bishops have been willing to admit that they made such contributions. Perhaps this is because large contingents of laity made it clear that if any diocesan funds were used to pay for an investigation of the Sisters (to whose defense the laity had sprung in large numbers by letter-writing campaigns to their bishops, to the apostolic delegate, to Cardinal Rodé, to the U.S. Bishops' conference, and even to the pope and by other means of showing their love and respect for the Sisters and their displeasure at the investigation), the usual contributions of these lay people to the dioceses would go elsewhere. Nothing of which I am aware has been said recently about who is paying for the investigation (a question in which many people, for various reasons, are very interested), but apparently it is not the Vatican, not the bishops or dioceses, not ordinary laity, and certainly not Religious congregations (many of which have also declined to pay the expenses, beyond hospitality and equipment at the site, of their on-site investigations). There is widespread suspicion that the money is coming from those wealthy and militantly traditionalist lay Catholics who have supported the resistance to Vatican II for decades.

Meanwhile, Phase Three, "on-site visitations" of selected congregations, was announced. Congregational leaders and some other people such as bishops were asked to nominate Religious to serve as on-site "visitors" or investigators, but the requirement that such persons make the recently revised "Profession of Faith" and "Oath of Loyalty" to the Holy See and agree to write secret reports on the congregations they "visited" led the vast majority of women Religious to decline to lend any active cooperation to such treatment of their fellow Religious. I have not heard that (and would be very surprised if) any congregational leaders have attempted to pressure members into such service. However, apparently a sufficient number of on-site investigators were sworn in, although some are apparently covering more than one assignment, and the on-site investigations began early in 2010. The second of the originally proposed three rounds of such events is currently under way. Apparently, the authorities have decided to cancel the third round.

While certain officials in the congregation are obliged to meet with the on-site visitors, any member can request such an interview. The right of members to confidential interviews with the visitors in an apostolic visitation is designed to provide an opportunity for members to report abuse, oppression, or irregularity in the congregation, especially on the part of superiors, without fear of intimidation or retaliation by those in power. Although there has been virtually no public discussion of the on-site experiences so far, there seem to be relatively few Sisters who feel any need or desire for individual interviews. And some who have requested them have, knowingly or unknowingly, turned the process inside out by using the interview to describe what they most appreciate about their congregations and their leadership. Two or three days seems to be more than adequate for the visitors to fulfill their duties, which conclude by their writing and submitting to Sister Millea their secret report on the congregation and shredding any material they collected on site.

The completion of the Phase Three "visits" will be followed by the preparation of Sister Millea's reports on the Institutes to the Vatican sometime in 2011. The Vatican has remained adamant, despite repeated requests and even strong objections by the congregations, that the reports—both those of the on-site investigators and those of Sister Millea—will remain secret. Congregations will not be allowed even to verify (much less rectify) the contents for factual accuracy, accidental or deliberate misinterpretation, or outright misrepresentation or lies. This secrecy of the reporting is perhaps the single most unacceptable aspect of the process for American Religious who have no categories in their legal or civil experience for anonymous (and therefore very possibly fraudulent and/or vindictively motivated) "evidence" or accusations being honored in any way by a just judiciary. The closest parallel from history is the medieval Inquisition in which those suspected of "heresy" in various forms were anonymously denounced to the Inquisitors who then tortured the accused until they "confessed" or executed them for refusing to do so. Joan of Arc, not incidentally a woman wearing clothes male hierarchs did not approve of and exercising leadership in a patriarchal Church and world, is the icon of this shameful period in Church history.

In this context of the negative escalation of the investigation in late 2009 into 2010 we can return to the issue that began to attract my attention as Sisters and others responded to the article on the history and character of ministerial Religious Life, namely, the profound disturbance so many Religious feel in the face of official ecclesiastical suspicion, distrust, disapproval, and even potential censure that is being clearly expressed, despite repeated verbal denials, by the form and content of the investigation.

Women Religious in the United States, from their arrival on these shores in the 1700s, through the founding of literally hundreds of non-enclosed congregations in the two centuries prior to the Council, were probably the most important factor in the establishment of the Roman Catholic Church in the United States. (The "Now You Know" media series offers two excellent courses, one by historian Margaret S. Thompson on the history of women's Religious Life in the United States and one by social historian Scott Appleby on the history of Catholicism in the United States that cover this topic in detail.) They have always far outnumbered the clergy. They built and staffed the educational, health care, and social service institutions that cared for the huge influx of mainly poor immigrants from Catholic countries who flooded into this country between the early 1800s and 1900s. Were it not for these institutions, which enabled the Church to keep its members more or less "segregated" from non-Catholic influences until they were sufficiently prepared to function as both Americans and Catholics in the broader society, it is hard to imagine that the Church could have sustained itself, much less become the significant institution in American culture that it has become. And it was Religious, for the most part, who facilitated the mainstreaming of Catholics into public life in the United States as well as fostering the vocations to the clergy that, until recently, permitted the development and maintenance of the vast diocesan structure that is currently unraveling.

In hindsight, it is clear that Sisters were inadequately, or not at all, remunerated for their service, leaving them in the precarious financial situation from which they suffer today. They had little or no influence, much less influence proportionate to their contributions, in ecclesiastical affairs. They lived in subjection, both in their private lives within their congregations and in their apostolates, to clerical and hierarchical power that was often intrusive and egregiously abused.

However, Sisters in general were venerated by the laity who saw them as "priests without portfolio" who often had more impact on the religious life of the laity than did the clergy. They were often the best educated women in the local Catholic community, trusted sources of religious knowledge and idealized models of Catholic spirituality. Even though they were sometimes justly feared for their overly strict discipline in overcrowded schools or their intractable "fidelity" to Church rules over people's real needs and were sometimes found stand-offish or elitist in their habited and cloistered exclusiveness and acceptance of privilege, Sisters in general were a highly respected and even beloved presence in the Catholic community and a respected face of that community among non-Catholics. Large numbers of young women, imitating the women Religious they knew, admired, and loved, flocked into the convent year after year, swelling the ranks in what we now realize was a somewhat abnormal and artificial "surge" of vocations that continues to create an unrealistic expectation of numbers today.

Even more important, in a way, was the fact that Religious were, even in the eyes of the hierarchy, the highest ranking women in the Church. Ecclesiastical officials knew that these women were doing a huge proportion of the Church's work, modeling its highest ideals, forming its younger generations, and in general keeping the ecclesiastical train on its tracks. Religious (Sisters and Brothers) were the only non-ordained who exercised quasi-official public ministry in the Church. Although often enough forced to defend themselves against, or find ways to live with, clerical and hierarchical oppression of all sorts (which is being documented today to the shock of even some Religious themselves), Religious were used to being seen as both superior to lay Catholics, especially women, in the ecclesiastical structure as well as in the spiritual life, that is, as "special" or even "elite" members of the Church as institution. In a very real way Religious experienced the validation of their lives in their special status as those called not only to a "higher vocation," to a "closer following" of Jesus, but also to a deeper participation in the official ministry of the Church, which excluded all women from the clergy.

In the wake of the Council with its clear articulation of the universal vocation of the baptized to "one and the same holiness," Religious had to come to grips theologically and spiritually with the fact that their vocation did not give them elite spiritual status within the People of God. This was certainly a—not the only—factor in the mass exodus of women from Religious Life in the aftermath of the Council. If this was not a "higher vocation," some reasoned, why make the sacrifices it entailed? But perhaps even more significantly, the Council's recognition that all the baptized are called by the sacraments of initiation to ministry as participants in the mission of Jesus, prophet, priest, and king, made the apostolates of women Religious no longer the only ministerial opening for lay people, especially women, in the Church. In short, if one could follow Christ as closely, and exercise all the ministries open to lay people, without making vows or living the discipline of Religious Life, why do so?

The Religious who stayed knew the answer to that question. The life was not about spiritual superiority or even about exclusive or privileged access to ministry. It was a response to a mysterious and personal call to a certain kind of commitment to Jesus Christ to the exclusion of any other primary life commitment and it found expression in the free choice of consecrated celibacy lived in community and ministry which constitutes the deepest reality of Religious Life.

However, what Religious have found deeply and permanently disturbing is the withdrawal, to a large extent, of the recognition, the positive approval of their life and ministry by the hierarchical Church. Religious were no strangers to the abuse of ecclesiastical power. But the sins of individual hierarchs is vastly different from blanket disapproval of the life itself and those who live it. This is a new experience for modern Religious, to be "personae non grata" in their own Church. Through long experience they had internalized the sense of being validated in their life and ministry by official recognition and approval as special and valued members of the institutional Church. Therefore, becoming objects of suspicion, disapproval, investigation, accusation, "doctrinal assessment," and various kinds of public reproof and repudiation, often precisely because of their exercise of their ministries, is experienced as a subversion of their persons and their lives. Being under siege as a problem in and to the Church they love and serve is profoundly unnerving and demoralizing.

This is the issue I wanted to address in the lengthy essay on "Religious Life as a Prophetic Lifeform," which is chapter 4 of this book. Religious Life has, almost from its inception, been recognized not simply as a "work force" in the Church but as a prophetic vocation. That identity was very clear when Religious Life emerged on the American frontier in an overwhelmingly Protestant, even anti-Catholic country. But the very meaning of "prophecy," to say nothing of a prophetic lifeform, became obscured as Religious were incorporated almost totally into the institutional agenda of the Church. For a hundred years before the Council a process of institutionalization, standardization, and even domestication muted to the point of virtual silence the specifically prophetic character of the life. Religious began to rediscover that important dimension of their identity as they emerged into public life by their increasing participation in social justice issues in the 1960s and their enthusiastic espousal in the Church of the agenda of Vatican II.

Intrinsic to the prophetic vocation within the Judaeo-Christian biblical tradition is the tension between prophecy and institution. Jesus was executed not because he did good works but because his doing of good works, like his preaching and teaching, was in the service of the liberation of the oppressed—those oppressed by secular power but especially those oppressed by religious power. Jesus was a quintessential prophet, a deeply committed Jew who was profoundly loyal to his religious tradition and, for that very reason, an implacable opponent of its perversion by the institutional power structure and its enforcers.

My purpose in the essay on Religious Life as a prophetic lifeform was to lay out in some detail the meaning of prophecy in our biblical tradition, describe what it looks like when it is active in the public sphere, analyze the tension and sometimes even opposition between those called to exercise the prophetic vocation and those whose role is maintaining order and exercising power within the institution. It is crucial, in my opinion, that Religious understand the ecclesiastical implications of the intrinsically prophetic character of our vocation and appropriate it with clarity and commitment.

Religious are not "mini-clerics," that is, agents of the institution. They are not a work force whose job is to indoctrinate or discipline their fellow believers. Their vow of obedience is made only to God. It is not the lay equivalent of the promise of obedience to hierarchical superiors made by the clergy at

ordination. It is, in fact, a commitment to continuous discernment within the context of their congregation of what God is
doing and asking in the current situation, which is sometimes
not only different from but opposed to what is "on the books"
of the official Church. Thus, a major theological challenge
that Religious must face is precisely the issue of obedience
which, for generations, has been interpreted as requiring total
submission to ecclesiastical authority. The accusation of "disobedience" is very painful for Religious, but facing it with theological clarity and moral courage is unavoidable if they are to
live faithfully the prophetic vocation to which they are called.

Like Jesus defending the woman taken in adultery
against the official interpretation and implementation of the
Law, the prophet today is not an automatic support system
for the institution's officials, a rubber stamp for their positions in all circumstances. In a Church in which a large proportion of the members find official Church teaching and
policy on numerous issues so burdensome, indeed morally
impossible, that they are leaving the Church in droves (see
the recent articles on the exodus of Catholics from the institutional Church by Cathleen Kaveny and Peter Steinfels in
Commonweal 137/8 [October 22, 2010]: 8, 16–20, respec-
tively), Religious will often find themselves reaching out to
the alienated, the excluded, the oppressed, not only in society but in the Church itself. They cannot expect that the officials of the institution are going to look favorably on this
prophetic activity any more than the Jerusalem hierarchy
looked favorably on Jesus' preferential interaction with tax
collectors and prostitutes. And, as execution was Jesus' fate,
Religious have to be prepared to resist, to the extent that
that is possible, but in any case to remain faithful to God, as
Jesus did, no matter what the cost.

One reason the prophetic vocation is so fraught with
suffering and danger is that it is not a theoretical engagement with abstract or timeless issues. It is a practical engage-

ment with concrete issues in the historical present. Religious are not under suspicion because they are debating the internal processions of the Trinity or the philosophical understanding of transubstantiation. They are on the front lines in regard to homosexuality, inter-religious dialogue, the identity and roles of women in the life and ministry of the Church, the realities of marriage and procreation within the framework of a patriarchal moral theology, mandatory singleness and sexual apartheid in ordained ministry that is causing eucharistic famine throughout the Church, ecclesiastical elitism and exclusivism in relation to other Christian traditions, intellectual freedom in theology and freedom of conscience in religion, and numerous other issues that the Vatican would like to declare "settled," or "closed," or "forbidden." Non-ordained Religious are perhaps the strongest professional voice in the Church able to call for honest and courageous approaches to these issues. But they cannot expect gratitude or approval from the institution for this engagement.

Perhaps the most "public" area of confrontation between Religious exercising their prophetic vocation and the ecclesiastical institution today concerns Vatican II. Religious, particularly women, were better prepared to understand the Council and as a group have been, since the close of the Council, the most theologically educated, publicly articulate, ministerially active, and energetic promoters of its spirit and content. Following the vacillating reign of Paul VI who was convinced of the Council's validity and direction despite his misgivings, John Paul II and Benedict XVI have resolutely pursued a restorationist agenda that has polarized the Church between those who long ardently for a return to the Tridentine era and those who have passionately espoused the conciliar renewal. This struggle cannot be finessed with the rhetoric of "continuity" and "rupture," and will not end any time soon. And, once again, Religious must accept that their fidelity to their own living of the conciliar renewal and their promotion of it in the Church and world will not endear them to the Curia or to the ultraconservative episcopacies that were created by John Paul II, much less to the magisterial fundamentalists among the laity.

This tension between, on the one hand, the prophetic vocation in the Church with its understanding of obedience as ongoing discernment of God's will in the signs of the times and its unwavering commitment to fulfilling that will with or without permission or approval of ecclesiastical officials, and, on the other hand, the institutional hierarchy with its claim to be the sole true representative, interpreter, and enforcer of God's will, is not the exclusive province of women Religious nor is it new on the ecclesiastical agenda. What is, to some extent, new is that it is now "out in the open" and non-ordained Religious are a symbolic, and therefore easily identifiable, representative of it. Intimidating and silencing Religious is a warning to any Catholic whose life or ministry poses a challenge to official positions. If it can happen to the nuns, it can happen to anybody.

Once again, after the publication of this long essay on Religious Life as prophetic, Richard McBrien summarized it for *NCR* readers who would not have time for or interest in reading the whole of it. And a very welcome, courageous support of its spirit and content came, unsolicited, from a Redemptorist, who with unpretentious simplicity described himself as "a religious, who happens to be called to ministry and service as a bishop in the church and world," Kevin Dowling, CSsR, the Ordinary of Rustenburg, South Africa. This member of the hierarchy who has devoted so much of his episcopal life to the prophetic task of meeting the AIDS crisis in South Africa embodies the hope that one day the charisms of prophecy and institutional leadership will function in a more complementary way than they have in most of the history of the Church.

I have little doubt that, consciously or unconsciously, the tension in the contemporary Church which is focused by, but definitely not limited to, the struggle over the Council is what is really at the base of the current investigation of Religious. Getting Religious back in male-mandated dress, officially enclosed houses, institutional apostolates controlled by the clergy, under the control of compliant superiors who see themselves as delegates of the hierarchy are expressions of a deeper agenda, namely, the neutralizing of the prophetic role of Religious in the Church. In our time, that neutralization is in the service of the reversal of the conciliar renewal. As I try to suggest in the conclusion of this book, there are a variety of ways to look at this situation and its possible outcomes. But nothing constructive can be built on denial of what is actually going on. We can build a house for Wisdom only on the bedrock of truth.

CHAPTER ONE

"WE'VE GIVEN BIRTH TO A NEW FORM OF RELIGIOUS LIFE"

Author's Note: The following is not and never was an article nor intended for publication. It originated as a spontaneous response in an e-mail conversation among a few colleagues. It became public without my knowledge and, in response to numerous requests for its publication, I have edited it slightly for purposes of clarity and allowed the National Catholic Reporter *to make it available to readers.*

Dear Colleagues,

   Thanks for your e-mails.

   I am not inclined to get into too much of a panic about this "visitation," which is really an investigation. We just went through a similar investigation of seminaries, equally aggressive and dishonest. I do not put any credence at all in the claim that this is friendly, transparent, aimed to be helpful, etc. It is a hostile move and the conclusions, I'm sure, are already in. It is meant to be intimidating. But I think if we believe in what we are doing (and I definitely do) we just have to be peacefully about our business, which is announcing the Gospel of Jesus Christ, fostering the Reign of God in this world.

We cannot, of course, keep them from investigating. But we can receive them, politely and kindly, for what they are, uninvited guests who should be received in the parlor, not given the run of the house. When people ask questions they shouldn't ask, the questions should be answered accordingly. I just hope we will not, as we American Religious so incline to do, think that by total "openness" and efforts to "dialogue" we are going to bring about mutual understanding and acceptance. There is nothing mutual about this process, and it is not a dialogue. The investigators are not coming to understand—believe me, we found that out in the seminary investigation. So, let's be honest but reserved, supply no "ammunition" that can be aimed at us, be non-violent even in the face of violence, but not be naïve. Non-violent resistance is what finally works as we've found out in so many arenas.

In my work on the renewal of Religious Life over the last eight years I have come to the conclusion that congregations like ours, the kind represented by LCWR in this country, have, in fact, birthed a new form of Religious Life. We are really no longer "congregations dedicated to works of the apostolate"—that is, monastic communities whose members "go out" to do institutionalized works basically assigned by the hierarchy as an extension of their agendas, e.g., in Catholic schools and hospitals, etc. We are ministerial Religious. Ministry is integral to our identity and vocation. It arises from our baptism specified by profession, discerned with our congregational leadership and effected according to the charism of our congregation, not by delegation from the hierarchy. We are not monastics at home. We are not extensions of the clergy abroad. Our whole life is affected by our ministerial identity: searching out the places (often on the margins of the Church and society) where the need for the Gospel is greatest (which may be in Church institutions but often is not); living in ways that are conducive to our ministry; preaching the Gospel freely as Jesus commissioned his itinerant, full-time companions to do. Our community life and ministries are corporate but not "common life" in the sense of everyone being in the same place at the same time doing the same thing.

The phase of post-conciliar "updating" for us was brief. We realized, by our return to the Gospel and to our own foundations, that we were called to much more radical (meaning in-depth) renewal than surface adjustments of lifestyle. There is no going back. But I think we may have to claim this, calmly and firmly, in the face of this now organized effort to get us back into the older form. We are as different from pre-conciliar "congregations devoted to works of the apostolate" such as those represented by CMSWR—of whom the Vatican is much more approving—as the mendicants were from the Benedictine monks. The big difference is that the pre-conciliar type of apostolic congregations read *Perfectae Caritatis* [conciliar Decree on the Up-to-date Renewal of Religious Life] and did what it asked: deepened their spirituality (I hope), and did some updating—shorter habits, a more flexible schedule, dropping of customs that were merely weird, etc. We read *Perfectae Caritatis* through the lenses of *Lumen Gentium* [Dogmatic Constitution on The Church] and *Gaudium et Spes* [Pastoral Constitution on the Church in the Modern World]. We were called out of the monastic/apostolic mode of world abandonment and into the world that *Gaudium et Spes* declared the Church was embracing after centuries of rejection.

There is no problem, as I see it, with CMSWR-type communities continuing the older form if that is what they feel called to do. Benedictinism didn't disappear when the Franciscans were founded. There is only a problem if they feel called to halt the journey we are on. That's where, in my view, we just have to be as courageous as our forebears like Angela Merici [founder of the Ursulines] and Mary Ward [founder of the Lorettos] and Nano Nagle [Presentation of the Blessed

Virgin Mary] and Marguerite Bourgeoys [Congrégation de Notre Dame] and Mary MacKillop [Josephites] and Louise de Marillac [Daughters of Charity] and all those other pioneers of apostolic Religious Life long before it was officially approved in 1900. The institutional Church has always resisted the new in Religious Life, especially among women. But the new will continue to happen. At this moment in history, we are it. So, let's be what we are: women Religious who are not cloistered and ministers who are not ordained. Canon law has no categories yet for that combination in a distinct lifeform. But we exist. Law follows life, not vice versa.

On the subject of the Stonehill "symposium" [held at Stonehill College, 2008, and very critical of LCWR-type congregations]—it wasn't really a symposium where people come together to share diverse views in the effort to reach greater truth. It was a pep rally for those convinced they are right and can only be right if people not like them are wrong. They were listening to themselves. That's fine—provided they don't go after other people. We are not after them. This is a fake war being stirred up by the Vatican at the instigation of the frightened. Let's not get into it. Also, what is the worst thing than can happen from this investigation? They are surely not going to shut down 95 percent of the Religious congregations in this country, even if they'd like to, any more than they closed all the seminaries that were not teaching nineteenth-century moral theology or buying the official line that the clergy sex abuse scandal was caused, not by corrupt bishops protecting pedophile priests, but by homosexual seminarians (who were not even born when most of the abuse was taking place).

Well, that's where I am on this. I refuse to go into a panic over this "visitation." There are better things to do. Always glad to hear from any of you on any of this.

Peace and courage,
Sandra

CHAPTER TWO

WHY THEY STAY(ED)

Women Religious and the Apostolic Visitation

Two sets of questions concerning U.S. women Religious are roiling the waters in and outside the Church today: (1) Why are Religious disturbed about the Apostolic Visitation? (2) What is the real motivation for this investigation?

WHY ARE RELIGIOUS DISTURBED ABOUT THE VISITATION?

Some laity, and even some (mostly more conservative) Religious, wonder why Religious would be upset at the invitation of Vatican officials to a discussion of their life with a view to encouraging and supporting the quality of Religious Life today. After all, no life is perfect and sometimes helpful outsiders can see things insiders miss.

Many Religious (members and leaders) as well as Catholic laity and some priests and bishops are disturbed by the Apostolic Visitation currently being conducted for two reasons: the *fact* of the investigation and the *mode* of the investigation.

The fact: Religious congregations (sometimes called "orders" or "communities") are in regular dialogue with

Church authority. The officers of the Leadership Conference of Women Religious (LCWR), which represents, through their leaders, about 95 percent of Religious congregations in the United States meet, on their own initiative, annually in Rome with the officers of Congregation for Institutes of Consecrated Life and Societies of Apostolic Life (CICLSAL), the Vatican bureau concerned with Religious Life, for the purpose of such dialogue, and they make strenuous (often unreciprocated) efforts to create open communication (see documentation on the LCWR website). Heads of orders are in regular contact with local ordinaries and most orders invite the local bishop to visit on various occasions. They must, and do, consult with the bishop and/or pastor when there are concerns about the ministry of Religious in a diocese or parish.

Furthermore, Religious Life, including the behavior of its members, is no longer hidden in cloistered dwellings but is reasonably open to the view of both laity and clergy. Some people, lay or cleric, might prefer Religious to wear atemporal uniforms of homespun and sensible oxfords rather than simple contemporary professional clothes, or to live in special dwellings and teach in a parish school rather than living, perhaps individually or intercongregationally (as some Religious have since the first century) or at a distance from their headquarters (as missionaries always have), in relation to their now diverse and widespread ministries. But there is nothing intrinsic to Religious Life about a particular type of clothing or dwelling or ministry. Clothing of Religious, according to the directives of Vatican II, is to be simple, modest, hygienic, and appropriate to the times; housing is to be appropriate to the form of community life and poverty specified in an order's approved documents (called "constitutions"); ministries are to be undertaken in obedience as obedience is understood in those same documents. These norms are applied differently by different orders and this has always been the case, often enough even among houses of a single order. Jesus and his itinerant band of ministerial disciples wore no special clothes and had no fixed abode. He brought down the murderous ire of the hierarchy of his own religious tradition because, among other things, he related to women as equals and involved them along with men in his ministry, reached out to the "disordered" and marginalized in his society, laid healing hands on the suffering, conversed with and allowed himself to be challenged and changed by people outside his own religious tradition, refused to condemn anyone, however "sinful," except religious hypocrites burdening people with obligations beyond their strength.

The current "Apostolic Visitation" is not a normal dialogue between Religious and Church authorities. It is the ecclesiastical analogue of a Grand Jury indictment, set in motion when there is reasonable suspicion, probable cause, or a *prima facie* case of serious abuse or wrongdoing of some kind. There are currently several situations in the U.S. Church that would justify such an investigation (widespread child sexual abuse by clerics, episcopal cover-ups of such abuse, long-term sexual liaisons by people vowed to celibacy, embezzlement of Church funds, cult-like practices in some Church groups), but women Religious are not significantly implicated in any of these. Religious are disturbed by the implied accusation of wrongdoing that *the very fact* of being subjected to an apostolic visitation involves, especially because the "charges" are vague or non-existent. We will return to this point in regard to the second question about motivation.

The mode: The characteristics of a Grand Jury indictment process (which have led most modern Western countries to abolish the Grand Jury as a judicial instrument) are that the Grand Jury can compel witnesses to testify under oath; proceedings are secret; defendants and/or their counsel may not hear the witness against them.

A number of features of the current investigation of Religious are problematic or repugnant to intelligent, educated, adult women in Western society. For example, even though the visitation had been authorized well before the annual meeting of the LCWR officials with CICLSAL in Rome in late 2008, the forthcoming visitation was not even hinted at during that meeting. The Religious leaders discovered that their orders and members were under investigation by reading about it in the secular press. Many Religious experienced this, rightly or wrongly, as an expression of contempt for them and especially for their leaders. And Americans could hardly not see this tactic as a kind of "sting" operation in which enforcement personnel raid suspects who are already deemed guilty, using the element of surprise to prevent escape, hiding of evidence, or defense. Religious are not trying to escape since they are all in Religious Life by their own choice. The evidence of the quality of their lives is the hospice patients they comfort, the students they teach, the directees and retreatants they counsel, the poor they feed, the sick they nurse, their peace work and justice advocacy, the research and art they produce. They do not feel that their carrying out of Vatican Council II's directives in the renewal of their lives and their resulting presence to and ministry in the world for which Jesus died needs defense.

In other words, whatever the Vatican may have intended, the initiation of this "visitation" was calculated to appear to many Americans, Catholic and others, inside and outside Religious Life, not as an invitation to respectful and fruitful dialogue and ongoing improvement of their lives but as an unwarranted surprise attack. One Religious speaking to me referred to it as "the Pearl Harbor model of dialogue."

Apostolic visitations, precisely because they imply suspicion if not guilt, are typically undertaken in regard to specific groups, such as a Religious order, province, or monastery, a diocese, a particular pious society, or particular practices or behaviors, such as suspect cults or fraudulent claims of apparitions or private revelations and so forth. This investigation, however, targeted indiscriminately all sixty thousand or more U.S. women Religious in some four hundred orders. It would be equivalent to setting out to investigate all sacramentally married people in the United States or all the priests and bishops of every diocese in the country. Undoubtedly some abuses could be found in any such global group, as they probably can be among Religious. But the implication that whatever abuse is being investigated is so widespread and deep rooted among Religious that all of them must be investigated is deeply disturbing if not insulting. These women, who have no obligation to be or remain Religious, have given thirty, forty, fifty, sixty, even seventy years of their lives in largely unremunerated service to the Church and its members. What could possibly justify such universal suspicion?

Religious then learned that a single "visitator" had been appointed, without any consultation, for the entire population. Her competence might indeed be astounding. But she was an unknown among U.S. women Religious who include in their number a virtual "hall of fame" of outstanding, highly credible women who might have been tapped for this sensitive role. The visitator is unknown because she has spent a good part of her mature Religious Life outside this country and belongs to a small order with one small province in the United States. But could any one person, however talented and experienced, no matter what group she belonged to, questioning subjects without the presence of any witnesses and rendering secret reports, which the subjects may not verify even for accuracy much less "tone" or "inference," possibly carry out a task of such scale and scope? Nevertheless, leaders of Religious orders made good faith efforts to cooperate with a process that is hardly comprehensible to people not living in a totalitarian political system.

They then found out that Phase Three of the investigation would involve "site visitations" (of congregations chosen by the single investigator) by teams composed by the single investigator from a pool of nominees who had to swear a loyalty oath, not to the people being investigated whose reputations and ministries were at stake, but to the investigating authority (the Holy See). Superiors were invited to submit names of candidates for these teams. Understandably, many Religious—congregations as a whole, superiors, and individual Religious—declined the invitation to make any kind of loyalty oath to any human being (they have all made lifelong vows to God, which they consider quite adequate) or to investigate their fellow Religious and write secret reports about them. The solidarity among women Religious, both within their own orders and among orders, is too deep for many to even contemplate participation in such a process. But that leaves open the unsettling possibility or even likelihood that those who are willing to become site visitators will have views of Religious Life, authority, and justice quite different from those they investigate.

Furthermore, the orders selected for site visitations have been asked to pay the transportation and other expenses of those sent to investigate them! Each successive element of the visitation has elicited more gasps of shock and disbelief from American women used to a legal system that, despite its grave flaws, espouses transparency, protects the rights of the accused, and is based on an assumption of innocence.

Most recently the *Instrumentum Laboris* or working document for the second phase has appeared. All heads of orders will be required to answer in writing a long, detailed questionnaire that will surely consume a great deal of valuable time that congregational leaders should be devoting to their very heavy primary responsibilities: spiritual leadership of their congregations, fostering community, supporting ministry, caring for their members both active and infirm, and trying to handle the enormous financial challenges facing most orders today. Furthermore, every individual Religious is being asked to reflect on this same list of questions. Most (probably all) congregations frequently spend quality time, individually and corporately, in reflection and examination of their life, on planning and implementation of processes for the improvement of the quality of their lives and ministries, and on decision making for their immediate and long-range futures. Being asked to address a list of "one-size-fits-all" questions is not only a consumption of valuable personal, community, and ministerial time and energy but implies that Religious have been living in a state of superficial distraction or self-delusion from which they need to be awakened by mandated self-examination. Most women Religious will tell anyone who asks that they spend a great deal of time and energy in serious reflection on their personal spiritual life (in daily prayer, annual and more frequent retreats, spiritual direction, personal discernment of life and ministry with their community and its leadership, ongoing education) and their corporate life in community and ministry (in congregational days, assemblies, chapters, small group meetings, council meetings, community discernment processes, and so on). These inquiries run much deeper than the mechanical questions on the *Instrumentum.*

At the end of all this investigation, including the site visitations of Phase Three, the single investigator will (apparently without the help of anyone) synthesize all this material and write a comprehensive secret report on the whole of ministerial Religious Life in this country for the Vatican. Women Religious are professionals who are very familiar with assessments and evaluations of their institutions such as schools, hospitals, and social service agencies and certification processes for personnel including themselves. Such professionals could not imagine appointing, for example, a single chemistry professor from a foreign university to evaluate single-handedly all the universities in the United States (programs, professors, administration, finances, libraries and laboratories, admissions processes, graduation and placement statistics, extracurricular activities, student life, etc.), judge them all, and prepare a secret report for the Department of Health, Education, and Welfare on their "quality." Religious orders are extremely diverse in foundation, history, charism, purposes, personnel, government, traditions, problems, financial resources, ministries, community life, spirit, and so on. Even if the report gets things basically right about one order, how applicable would that be to the others? To many, this investigation appears, at the very least, astonishing, if not downright mind-boggling in the unprofessionalism of its process.

In short, not only does the fact of the investigation feel threatening if not sinister but its mode is upsetting to adult professional women Religious.

WHAT IS THE MOTIVATION FOR THE VISITATION?

The motivation for the visitation remains very vague. Perhaps the most commonly voiced hypothesis of both lay people and Religious is that the purpose of the investigation is to ascertain the size and status of the financial assets of Religious orders of women in order to enable the U.S. bishops to take possession of those assets to pay their legal debts. Even if there is no validity to this hypothesis (and I dearly hope that that is the case), it is distressing that Catholics' confidence in their hierarchy has been so eroded that they suspect their bishops of wishing to further impoverish Religious orders struggling to support their elderly and infirm members. Another frequently voiced hypothesis, with perhaps more credibility, is that Cardinal Rodé, the head of CICLSAL, wants to mandate for all women Religious a return to pre-conciliar lifestyles akin to those in his eastern European homeland under Communism. Again, the suspicion is not without some basis in remarks the cardinal has made publicly, but there is no proof of such an intention and, in any case, such a move would surely occasion far more trouble than the Vatican probably wants to deal with.

The only "purpose" stated in the official documents is "to look into the quality of the life of women religious in the United States who are members of apostolic religious institutes." At several junctures Cardinal Rodé, who initiated the investigation, has suggested that his concern is about the "decline in numbers" of Religious in these orders. There seems to be an implied "cause and effect" relation between these two concerns, namely, that the decline in numbers is somehow due to the poor quality of the life of Religious. It is time to address this implication with some facts.

It is true that the numbers of U.S. women Religious declined precipitously, by tens of thousands, from the high point (at least 120,000) in the mid-sixties to something around 60,000 today. This was due principally to two factors, not identical, namely, the sharp drop-off in numbers entering Religious Life and a major exodus of professed Religious from the life. These phenomena were largely simultaneous, which leads many people to fail to distinguish between them.

Numbers entering: The inflation of numbers of Religious from the late 1940s to the 1960s paralleled the influx of large numbers of men following Thomas Merton into monasteries in the disordered social aftermath of World War II. This brief period of heightened religious enthusiasm has been studied extensively and I will not engage this data here. Suffice it to say that, prior to the vocational tsunami beginning in the 1940s and peaking in the mid-1960s, the total number of women Religious, between the 1700s when the first ones came to this country and the early 1900s, was nowhere near the post-war high point. Indeed, it was closer to today's "low point." To understand the sudden decline in entrants after 1965 one has to understand the sudden inflation immediately after the war. I will mention here only the most important factors.

Pre–*Humanae Vitae* Catholic families tended to be large, often five to ten children. The U.S. bishops insisted that parents were morally obliged to send those children to Catholic schools, which were almost totally staffed by the unpaid workforce of women Religious. Thus the average Catholic girl spent most of her waking hours for eight to twelve years in the company of "the nuns," becoming familiar with their life, admiring them as "special" people, as the favorites of God and male authority figures in the Church, as uniquely powerful women who were more educated and professionally engaged than most other women they knew. The nuns wore fascinating and exotic clothes, lived in mysterious enclaves whose interiors "seculars" could only imagine, and seemed to enjoy a special *esprit de corps* among themselves in their secret world.

At that point in time the Catholic girl had two viable life options when she completed high school (or more rarely college): to marry like her mother and begin her own life of child rearing or enter the convent. While by far the majority chose marriage (probably as naïvely as the minority chose Religious Life!), the numbers from every graduating class entering the convent was impressive. And parents, trained to regard a "vocation" in the family as an honor and blessing, could afford to offer one or more children to God without fear of dying without grandchildren. Novitiate classes could number thirty in a small congregation to a hundred or more in a large one. And Catholic culture made leaving the convent after profession as unthinkable as divorce.

Post–*Humanae Vitae* (ironically, this document reiterating the ban on "artificial contraception" seemed to precipitate, or at least not prevent, a sharp decrease in the Catholic fertility rate) Catholic families are as small as those of most other Americans, that is, one or two children. The number of Catholic schools rapidly declined. Even those which existed usually had few or no Sisters in the classroom. Parents claimed their right to send their children to the schools of their choice, often choosing a better-endowed or geographically closer public school over a Catholic one. Feminism and other forces combined to open opportunities to girls well beyond the "marriage or convent" choice. There was no profession or ministry open to a woman Religious that was not equally open to a lay woman. Parents who wanted grandchildren were less inclined to promote their (often only) daughter's choice of the convent. Church officials were rapidly closing the "feeder" institutions (Catholic schools) and Religious orders were losing their high schools to economic and personnel pressures.

The bad news in all this, of course, was that by the mid-sixties very few Catholic girls considered Religious Life and even fewer entered. The good news is that the only real reason, now, for a young woman to enter was that she really felt called by God to a life of consecrated celibacy lived with others who shared this vocation and expressed in a total commitment to the service of God's people. Not having a husband or children, not becoming personally wealthy, perhaps not being able to pursue exactly her professional interests were no longer seen as just "part of the package" of an otherwise "special" and therefore rewarding vocation but as difficult, free choices of a highly demanding life which could find justification only in a genuine Religious vocation. Women took considerably longer to come to such decisions. The huge novitiate classes of eighteen-year-olds disappeared, and women entering tended to be in their late twenties or thirties or even older, applying not as "classes" or "bands," but as individuals. This had little to do with the quality of Religious Life. It had everything to do with there being far fewer Catholic children to begin with. They were not exposed to Religious Life (or, often, even to normal Catholic culture within which a Religious vocation might seem normal or attractive); opportunities for women had broadened enormously; parents tended not to encourage vocations; women were putting off life-commitment decisions for a decade or more beyond high school.

Religious leaving: Beginning in the late 1960s and up through the 1980s there was a massive exodus of women from Religious Life. There were certainly some who left in bitterness and anger at what they considered an alienating and oppressive life of uniformity and repression in which they had somehow become trapped. But the vast majority, many of whom continue to this day to maintain warm relationships with their former orders and convent classmates, left because they came to realize that they were not called to Religious Life. Many realized that they were called to marriage and that celibacy was not required for holiness or for engagement in ministry which was, for many, the main reason they had entered. Others wanted careers, financial independence, or personal autonomy incompatible with Religious poverty, obedience, and community. The new theology of vocation and moral freedom and responsibility encouraged by the Council made the once "unthinkable" (i.e., change of state of life) thinkable. The stigma attached to "leaving the convent" largely vanished, making the change culturally acceptable.

These women, part of the great influx of the 1950s and 1960s, were now in their twenties, thirties, or forties, generally well educated and professionally prepared for a world and Church that now had much more room for lay, including female, participation. Many of the thousands of women who left Religious Life within a couple decades of entering remain to this day profoundly grateful for the psychological, spiritual, and professional formation they received in Religious Life. They are not sorry they entered and do not consider their convent experience a "mistake" or those years of their lives "wasted." But they are also glad that they realized in time that they were not called to that life and that it was possible for them to peacefully follow God's will in leaving as they had followed that will, as they understood it, when they entered.

The combination of many departures and few entrants has created a "gap" between age twenty and age fifty through ninety in most orders. This creates problems for women entering today who have few peers and few Religious right ahead of them. No one underestimates the seriousness of this situation and efforts like "Giving Voice" (a cross-congregational association of younger Religious) and intercongregational formation programs are trying to address it. But it is important to realize that neither the exodus from Religious Life nor the decline in numbers entering was due to a sudden deterioration in the quality of Religious Life. The change in demographics, in the sociology of the Catholic sub-culture, in theology of states of life and vocation, in roles of women in Church and society, and many other factors we cannot delve into here created the situation with which we are contending today.

That situation, in my opinion and that of most Religious I know, is indeed challenging but not desperate. Nor will it be rectified by a retroversion to pre-conciliar convent lifestyles or disciplinary initiatives of Vatican authorities. The response, which is and will continue to be arduous, lies with those who have stayed.

CONCLUSION: THE ONES WHO STAYED

A far more interesting question than who left and why is, "Why did the ones who stayed, stay?" These are the women who, today, compose the largest cohort in Religious Life, the sixty- to eighty-year-olds. This is not only the largest but also the most vibrant group in Religious Life, flanked at one end with a small number of wonderfully courageous new entrants in their late twenties to forties and at the other end by a still numerous group of women in their nineties and beyond who continue to witness with stunning beauty to the joy and fruitfulness of a life totally given to God and God's people. The members of this largest cohort are examples of "eighty being the new sixty." Generally in vigorous mental, psychological, and physical health, many have to take time off from full-time ministries to celebrate their fiftieth and sixtieth anniversaries in Religious Life. They are carrying the responsibilities of leadership in their orders and supporting with indomitable hope and courage the Church-wide but beleaguered effort to keep the spirit and substance of Vatican II from succumbing to the tides of restorationism. These Religious are not hankering for the "good old days," for a return to special clothes and titles, instant recognition and elite status in Church and society, and someone to support them, think for them, and keep their life in order in a turbulent world. The real question is, who are these "stayers" and why did/do they stay?

These women are the contemporaries of those who left in the exodus of the 1970s and 1980s. Like those who left, they were young (in their twenties to forties), perhaps the best educated group of women in America at the time, professionally precocious, theologically well grounded, and becoming increasingly interdependently autonomous as women in the Church and world. These Religious were eminently well positioned to leave and had every reason (but one) to do so. They watched in anguish as increasing numbers of their friends made that choice. Religious Life had little to offer them, humanly or materially speaking. Orders were losing their big institutions; financial insecurity was becoming a major concern; few were entering. The institutional Church was repudiating feminism in all its forms; the papacy was engaged in vigorous restorationism; many in and outside the Church including some in Religious Life had resigned themselves to (or rejoiced in) what they saw as "the death of the Council" or the "end of renewal." The exciting theologies of liberation and lay ministerial empowerment in the Church were being repressed in favor of a renewed clericalism and centralization of power. From a strictly human standpoint it was a bleak time for those who had come of age in the joyous, Spirit-filled enthusiasm of the Council when community, equality of discipleship in the Church, commitment to the building of a better world, deepening spirituality, inter-religious dialogue, feminist empowerment were the very air they breathed. From every angle hope was being crushed and old world narrowness, neo-orthodoxy, and Vatican re-centralization were replacing the Spirit-filled, world-affirming, humane spirit of John XXIII and the Council.

In this crucible the ones who stayed were tested by fire. Elsewhere I have referred to and described in more detail this period as a corporate "dark night of sense and spirit" for women Religious. They were experiencing a deep purification of any sense of spiritual superiority (to say nothing of arrogant certainty), of elitism, of corporate power and influence, of "most favored status" or mysterious specialness in the Church. Their faith was being battered by profound theological tensions raised by the clash between what they most deeply, if obscurely, knew was true and what was happening in the Church and world. They had to find the taproot of their vocation, not in peer group euphoria, social status, or preferential treatment by the hierarchy, but in the core of their spirituality, face to face with the One to whom they had given their lives in celibate love, in the emptiness of a poverty that was spiritual as well as material, and in an obedience unto the death of everything they cherished, except the God in whom they believed. They found out experientially why Jesus withdrew to the mountains or the desert in the middle of the night and before dawn to pray, not to "set a good example" for the less spiritual but because he desperately needed God to make it through one more day.

As this cohort of women Religious made its way through the 1990s toward the new millennium, and even as financial and ecclesiastical problems multiplied, a serenity began to surface from the darkness. Even secular sociologists, but especially the laity who associate with these Religious and those they serve, have recognized that the joy and counter-intuitive confidence, the capacity for work and suffering, the whole-hearted commitment to their own spiritual lives and to the people to whom they minister, the unity and solidarity in community that is evident in most women's Religious congregations—given the enormity of the challenges they confront—must be rooted in something, Someone, much deeper and more central to their lives than anything temporal or material.

Some congregations have had to face their imminent demise and have begun to prepare, not to be passively wiped out by circumstances beyond their control, but, like Oscar Romero, to die into Christ's resurrection, leaving a legacy that will somehow rise in those they have loved and served. Many congregations have reconfigured their corporate lives by consolidation or merging or refounding and are launched into new adventures in a still strange land. Others, though diminished in size and resources, have decided that they can and will make it together into the future and have undertaken vigorous, faith-based strategic planning, including vocation work, to make that happen. But the important thing for our purposes here is that these women are still "staying" because, in the very core of their being, they do not just "belong to a Religious order"; they *are* Religious. Hopefully, the present investigation will make evident to those whose concerns gave rise to it the meaning of Religious Life as it is being envisioned, lived, and handed on today in congregations renewed in and by that Pentecostal outpouring of the Spirit called the Second Vatican Council.

CHAPTER THREE

DISCERNING MINISTERIAL RELIGIOUS LIFE TODAY

Its Past, Present, and Future

INTRODUCTION

In the distressing ferment generated by the Vatican investigation of U.S. women Religious one question has arisen repeatedly, in various forms, and been "answered," sometimes quite dogmatically, by people who have no lived experience of or academic competence in regard to Religious Life. Since the question is important, misinformation is not helpful to Religious themselves or to their many concerned lay friends, colleagues, and associates. The substance of the question is "What is 'apostolic Religious Life'?" But the question often takes the form of a three-pronged query about lifestyle: "Is culturally conspicuous, uniform garb (habit), fixed group dwelling from which members exit only by necessity and from which non-members are excluded (enclosure, cloister), and a daily schedule including shared meals, work, and especially the oral recitation of prescribed texts and vocal prayers, e.g., Divine Office, litanies, at several fixed times a day (horarium) essential to Catholic Religious Life as such?" The short answer is "no." But this answer requires historical, biblical, and theological expansion and support.

HISTORICAL OVERVIEW

Habit, enclosure, and horarium are not characteristic (much less essential) features of Religious Life as such but of one form of religious life, namely, monasticism. Virtually all literate religious/spiritual traditions throughout history and across the world include some form of monasticism, which itself pre-dates Christianity by millennia. Hinduism, Buddhism, Jainism, Judaism (e.g., the therapeutae), some classical Greek philosophical/religious traditions, Islam (Sufism) all include some form of monasticism, as do Protestantism, Anglicanism, Orthodoxy, and some ecumenical Christian movements as well as Catholicism. In all instances of monasticism the purpose of such features as habit (whether saffron robes, veils and scapulars, dervish tunics, shaved heads), enclosure (monasteries, convents), and horarium (involving chanting of sutras or psalms or recitation of devotional prayers, common meals, work, and the like), as well as such spiritual features as meditation and prayer, poverty, asceticism, celibacy, is to promote the spiritual perfection of the monastics, which is variously defined as enlightenment, nirvana, sanctification, contemplation, mystical union with God, return to the One, and so forth, through withdrawal from secular involvement and the practice of religious/spiritual observances.

Monasticism developed in Christianity in the fourth through fifth centuries CE in the East (under Pachomius in Egypt, Basil in Asia Minor, Cassian in Gaul) and in the sixth century in the West under Benedict of Nursia (480–547). Probably sometime between 530 and 560 Benedict wrote the great Rule from which most Western Christian monasticism derives. Prior to the development of the monastic life in

Christianity there were other forms of consecrated life that were non-monastic, such as professed consecrated virginity lived non-monastically within the early Christian communities and solitary hermit life in the desert.

Once it developed, the monastic version of Christian Religious Life was the predominant form in the Western Church from roughly 500 to 1500 CE but other forms also developed during that period, notably the military and hospitaler orders in the earlier Middle Ages and the mendicant form in the high Middle Ages. Neither of the latter were strictly monastic because an important feature in these new forms of Religious Life was itinerancy (traveling about) in the service of what we today would call apostolic work or ministry, that is, the expression of love of God through the service of the neighbor outside the monastic enclosure. Monastic stability, fostered and expressed by enclosure and horarium, was relativized by these newer forms to allow the Religious (e.g., the Templars, Franciscans) to travel about ministering in a variety of ways including nursing the sick, sheltering pilgrims, teaching in the new universities, advising at court and counseling the laity, preaching in the cities and countrysides, confronting emerging heresies, converting "pagans," etc.).

The most striking departure from the monastic model, beginning in the sixteenth century, occurred in the clerical apostolic orders/congregations such as the Jesuits and Redemptorists. The Jesuits in particular, by deciding that reciting the Divine Office in common was not compatible with their apostolic vocation, made the sharpest and most substantial break from monasticism. And by this time monastic habits in clerical orders had given way to more ordinary clerical or sometimes contemporary attire or were restricted to use in the house, and the dwellings of these Religious were not stable, enclosed monasteries but houses or residences among which members moved according to their ministries.

At this same time there was a powerful impetus among women to participate in the Church's expanding apostolate, which male Religious were exercising both in Europe and the Far East and in the New World. A number of efforts, by male and female founders, to create apostolic orders of women ran afoul of the requirement, absolutized by Boniface VIII in the papal bull *Periculoso* in 1298 and re-enforced by the Council of Trent, that all women Religious had to observe papal cloister under pain of excommunication. In other words, monasticism was the only recognized legitimate form of Religious Life for women.

This conviction that women had to be under male control (of father, husband, or hierarchy), should not appear alone or act in public, could not handle financial affairs without supervision, or even pursue their own spiritual lives without male permission and direction was theologized as God's will for women who were considered "the weaker sex" and therefore in need of physical, social, and spiritual protection for their own good and that of those (men) they might lead astray. But this patriarchal control agenda was, in fact, simply "baptized" cultural gender oppression, perhaps understandable in the Middle Ages but surely destined for historical demise. It is still in its death throes today and probably nowhere more visibly in the Western world than in the Catholic Church. Many people have expressed the suspicion that the current investigation of non-cloistered women Religious in the United States is another spasm in this misogynistic agenda.

The requirement of enclosure seriously impeded, without being able to completely subvert, the development of non-cloistered apostolic Religious Life among women. Some founders, like Vincent de Paul and Louise de Marillac (founders of the Daughters of Charity), declared their Sisters "not Religious" so that they could minister to the sick and poor outside of cloister. Others, like Angela Merici (Ursulines), Jane de Chantal and Francis de Sales (Visitandines), Joseph Medaille (Sisters of St. Joseph), Mary Ward (IBVM or Loretto Sisters), Nano Nagle (Presentation Sisters), Catherine McAuley (Sisters of Mercy), Mary MacKillop (Sisters of St. Joseph of the Sacred Heart), and many others, lived as and struggled to be recognized as Religious even while refusing to renounce their vocations to ministry. Some of these extraordinary pioneers of women's ministerial Religious Life were denounced for immorality, imprisoned, placed under interdict, and even excommunicated. Some orders were suppressed (in some cases only to resurrect later) while others were deflected from their founding charisms by reimposition of cloister. But these women, and the people they served, knew very well that, though not monastics, they were authentic Religious. And, despite unrelenting ecclesiastical opposition, they continued to live Religious Life, including the exercise—often impeded—of their apostolates, and to be accepted and appreciated as Religious by the people they served.

Finally, in 1900, Leo XIII, in the apostolic constitution *Conditae a Christo,* formally recognized as an authentic form of Religious Life non-cloistered "congregations devoted to works of the apostolate." This was not the creation by hierarchical fiat of a new form of Religious Life. It was the public recognition of a *fait accompli,* namely, that over the course of nearly four hundred years a new form of women's Religious Life had emerged, and its validity, already long recognized by the People of God and by civil governments (which often gave the apostolic groups the same civil privileges and exemptions they accorded cloistered monastics), required acknowledgment by the institutional church.

However, because of the struggle over cloister and its attendant monastic accoutrements (such as habit, horarium) women's apostolic Religious Life had developed as a hybrid phenomenon. Until the 1950s women Religious actually lived two different lives side by side: virtually the whole of monastic life at home and a full-time ministerial life in their apostolates. The typical non-stop seventeen-hour day—from 5:00 AM till 10:00 PM—in a pre–Vatican II convent involved modern women (dressed at all times in the restrictive fluting and pleats, floor-length gowns, starched wimples and veiled headdresses of seventeenth or eighteenth century peasants or nobles), struggling to "get in" to their daily schedule Mass, meditation, devotional vocal prayers, examen, some form of Divine Office, adoration of the Blessed Sacrament, the rosary, stations of the cross, and spiritual reading from assigned pious books as well as daily manual work assignments in the convent. They also participated daily (usually in silence) in three meals in common, with some role in their preparation and clean up, and spent an hour in common "recreation," which usually included handwork or mending, school work, parish or community tasks. Within the same day that included this full monastic routine they prepared classes and carried out a full day's professional schedule in school, hospital, or other Catholic institutions. They often taught catechism on the weekends and gave private lessons of various kinds to augment community income. In short, they carried all the burdens of the monastic life with none of the leisure for personal prayer, *lectio divina*, genuine community life, or ordinary recreation of monastics, and all the burdens of the apostolate without the professional preparation or privileges enjoyed by the clergy.

Between 1900, when their form of Religious Life was officially recognized, and the 1950s, when Pius XII launched

the process of renewal that eventually led to the changes following Vatican II, the already heavy demands of this double
life of "monastics at home" and "apostles abroad" intensi-
fied. Advanced professional education became increasingly
necessary and Catholic institutions staffed by Sisters multiplied rapidly. In the 1950s Pius XII urged Religious superiors
to begin the modernization of their congregations including
abolition of outmoded customs, humanization of the
lifestyle, increased attention to the professional and cultural
education of their Sisters, and the modification of practices
that were unhealthy for the Sisters or that alienated them
from their contemporaries. He specifically encouraged the
modification of habits which were, besides being outmoded,
often un-hygienic as well as expensive and which required
unreasonable amounts of time and energy to maintain. At
the same time the Sister Formation Movement in the United
States tackled the long overdue project of spiritual, intellectual, and psychological integration of Sisters through education in theology and philosophy as well as the humanities,
advanced professional preparation for competent ministry
in the modern world, and the deepening and increasing per-
sonalization of the spirituality of Sisters. The last was encouraged by the "House of Prayer Movement," which was primarily promoted by women's congregations and the directed
retreat movement originating with the Jesuits but enthusiastically embraced by women Religious.

At Vatican Council II council fathers like Cardinal Leon
Suenens vigorously promoted the agenda of renewal of
women's Religious Life. The Council directed congregations
to return to the biblical roots of their life and to the founding charisms (i.e., particular identifying graces) of their congregations. These charisms often included the apostolic visions and ministerial intentions of the founders. The
renewal was intended specifically to foster greater engage-

ment of women Religious with the modern world. Religious were urged not to restrict their apostolic zeal to the care of children, the sick, and the dying but to put their enormous gifts as educated modern women in the active and public service of the Reign of God by influential participation in all the spheres of life (social, economic, political, intellectual, artistic) that were bringing to birth a new cultural reality that would eventually be called globalized post-modernity.

Religious congregations entered into this process of renewal with typical energy and commitment and in a period of barely forty years they fairly well bridged the historical gap between their early modern European origins and post-modern American ecclesial and cultural reality. Given the glacial pace of most ecclesiastical development this renewal seemed to many, inside and outside Religious Life, to have taken place with shocking speed and suddenness. In fact, the removal of major (mostly monastic or purely cultural) barriers of all kinds made possible the full emergence of a new form of Religious Life that had been developing within and around those barriers for nearly four centuries, namely, non-monastic ministerial Religious Life for women.

The Council mandated for virtually all congregations a renewal chapter (an official congregational meeting for major decision making). These chapters extensively revised the Constitutions (rule of life) of the various orders and almost all of these revised Constitutions have since been approved by the Vatican. The rules of these congregations had traditionally stated, in various formulations, that the "primary end" of the life was "the perfection/sanctification of the members through withdrawal from the world and the practice of religious observances," that is, the living of the monastic life. They then gave, as a "secondary end," one or several specific apostolic work of the order, such as "the Christian education of youth" or "the care of the terminally ill."

Constitutions revised in response to the Council now typically define the purpose of the life as a single, integrated end in terms such as the following: "Urged by the love of Jesus Christ and empowered by his Spirit the Sisters incarnate their total vowed consecration to God in the promotion of God's Reign through a variety of ministries addressing the current needs of Church and society." These revised Constitutions then go on to describe how this integrated, contemplatively grounded, ministerial lifeform is to be lived among and by the Sisters.

Perhaps the most immediately visible, though hardly the most important, expression of this commitment to the broad and deep renewal of ministerial Religious Life was the relatively swift change in regard to the habit. Uniform dress was (and remains in many monastic groups) a feature of monastic life whose purpose is to suppress singularity, concern with appearance, vanity, and competition—even looking in a mirror or "reflecting surface" was a serious fault in pre-conciliar days!—so that the members of the monastery can pursue their common life without attracting the attention of each other or even themselves, living inconspicuously "hidden with Christ in God." This purpose had been inadvertently turned inside out as twentieth-century apostolic Religious, no longer cloistered, became more involved in modern life outside their convents. Their exotic "costumes" (as they were called in Europe) startled people on the street, created (intentionally or not) claims to special status and privileged treatment, and often made normal, egalitarian peer relationships difficult or impossible. A fully habited Religious in a grocery store, university classroom, or professional meeting was hardly inconspicuous!

The more extreme versions of floor-length robes, trains, voluminous sleeves, and veils descending from architectural headgear soon began to disappear, as the Council clearly intended. Most congregations then went through a relatively short period of experimentation with "modified habits" that often made their adult wearers feel (and look) like Catholic high school girls in uniform. One of Vatican II's stated criteria for the garb of Religious, besides hygiene, poverty, and simplicity, was "attractiveness." Increasingly, Sisters in ministerial orders questioned not only the attractiveness of their modified garb but the "witness value" of conspicuous dowdiness, especially in professional settings.

Within a relatively short time (and not without some embarrassing errors in judgment) most renewed congregations had successfully transitioned into simple contemporary dress appropriate to the now quite varied situations in their lives. They realized that clothes as such were neither "religious" nor "secular," did not make a person "holy" or "worldly," did not communicate anything that was not communicated by one's person, attitude, and behavior. Many discovered by experience that simple, unaffected, and appropriate contemporary dress quite effectively communicated what they wished to witness to: equality with and respect for their companions and the sincere desire to participate competently in contemporary culture without succumbing to the tyranny of fashion and consumerism. At this point, despite the sometimes overheated agitation around the "habit issue" on the part of some traditionalists, the issue of clothing is no longer high (or at all) on the agenda in most congregations. By far the majority of mature Religious in the United States wear contemporary clothes; most lay people seem quite comfortable with this; and no one seems to object to any congregation or individual Religious wearing traditional or modified monastic garb if they choose to do so.

If the habit was the emotional flash point of renewal, the broadening of and full commitment to ministry, finally liberated from the monastic constraints under which it had labored for centuries, was the spiritual substance at the heart of renewal. A major transition was under way, from ecclesiastically delegated and controlled apostolates of caring for Catholics in large Catholic institutions attached to monastic-style convents to more individualized ministries in situations of need regardless of the denominational affiliation or lack thereof, ability to pay, or respectability of the recipients.

Sisters became hospital and prison chaplains, poverty and immigration lawyers, and medical professionals of all kinds. They assumed ministries in parishes that were increasingly without sufficient clergy. They became tutors of at-risk youth and adults who needed to learn English. They undertook hospice care, plunged into political advocacy and peace work and staffed NGOs, assumed leadership in the promotion and defense of women, served on boards of non-profits, addressed homelessness in a variety of ways. They became skilled spiritual and retreat directors and founded or staffed spirituality centers. They started alternate schools for the disadvantaged and reached out to AIDS victims, street people, the addicted, and the societally or ecclesiastically rejected. They became theologians and artists, scientists and researchers. Their previous living situations (convents or monasteries) ceased to determine what ministries they could undertake; rather, the ministries they undertook began to determine where and how they lived. (As we will see shortly, this move is deeply rooted in the Gospel.)

Living singly, intercongregationally, or in small mobile groups in function of the ministries in which they were involved furthered the dismantling of the monastic lifestyle. Ministerial Religious were no longer enclosed monastics following a horarium that demanded their prolonged presence in the convent several times a day. The demise of the routine of vocal prayers in common and uniform devotional life demanded the development by every Sister of a serious personal commitment to a life of contemplative and shared prayer. Unsustained by a fixed program of "observances," she had to develop a prayer life deep and intense enough to nourish her more demanding ministerial commitment and the relationship with God in which it was rooted and that it expressed. New ways of *being* and *living* community have had to be developed in place of "living in" community geographically and physically, which any who have lived this way know is no guarantee of genuine affective and effective sharing of life.

These changes in the way of life of ministerial Religious have been radical (in the sense of root deep) and extremely challenging. And we have certainly not found completely adequate solutions to some of these challenges. But most renewed congregations—and most individual Religious who have persevered through the traumatic decades of renewal—are firmly convinced that, no matter how serious the challenges or how many mistakes are made in dealing with them, this new form of Religious Life that they are living today is that to which they are and have been called since the foundation of this lifeform centuries ago. Gospel fidelity to their vocation requires that there be "no turning back," no fearful security seeking in a re-monasticizing of their life, no surrender to external or internal control agendas no matter where they originate. Ministry has moved from its peripheral position as a "secondary end" of Religious Life, a controlled and restricted "overflow" of the monastic "primary end," to the very center of the self-understanding and commitment of women Religious. The first and second commandment have become one for them. Love of God and loving service of God's people are no longer juxtaposed projects competing for their time and energy. They are the inhaling and exhaling of one life totally consecrated to God by perpetual profession of the vows and poured out in total self-gift in ministry that is not restricted to prayer or even specified ministries in Catholic institutions.

BIBLICAL AND THEOLOGICAL CONSIDERATIONS

Important as it is to realize what ministerial Religious Life is *not*, namely, monastic life or a hybrid combination of monastic life and ecclesiastically mandated institutional tasks, and therefore what is not essential to it, namely, monastic characteristics such as habit, enclosure, and horarium, it is much more important to understand what this life is. Unlike monasticism, which is a feature of virtually all literate religious/spiritual traditions, there is no analogue outside Christianity for ministerial Religious Life. Doing good to one's neighbor according to one's means is, of course, integral to virtually all religions but only Christianity has developed an organic lifeform in which the whole of a person's life is taken up, by profession of perpetual vows, to the exclusion of all other primary life commitments such as family or profession or project, into a love of God that expresses itself in complete self-giving to the neighbor.

Christianity is the continuation in this world of the life of Jesus who came to pour out his life for the salvation of humanity, to inaugurate the Reign of God on earth as in heaven. One might say that the originality of Christianity consists in the unification into one single movement of the two great commandments of the Law, love of God with one's whole being and love of all human beings as oneself, not as a human project of benevolence but as the ongoing enactment of God's project in Jesus: God so loved the world as to give God's only Son that all might have eternal life (see Jn 3:16). Ministerial Religious Life is, in other words, an original Christian lifeform radically focused on the coming of the Reign of

God, not the Christian form of a more widespread religious phenomenon of self-transcendence. (The Christian form of monasticism, of course, is Christian precisely because of and to the extent that commitment to Jesus' salvific project is integral to the prayer life of its members, but monasticism is not our topic here.) To understand ministerial Religious Life, therefore, we can look only to the New Testament for its model. It is a particular kind of discipleship of Jesus.

All Jesus' disciples are called to participate in one way or another in his mission of the transformation of humanity (as well as non-human creation) in God. The pre-Easter Jesus had many kinds of disciples. Some, like Martha, Mary, and Lazarus of Bethany (see Lk 10:38–42; Jn 11:5), were householders who followed Jesus within the context of loving family life. Others, like Zacchaeus (Lk 19:2–9) or the royal official (Jn 46–54), followed him by just and generous involvement in secular occupations. But there was one rather small group of women and men (see Lk 8:1–3) whom Jesus called to abandon everything—home or fixed abode of any kind, family of origin, marriage and progeny, all personal property, occupation or profession—to be in his company on a 24/7 basis, to take on in real time his itinerant form of life, to participate in his daily full-time ministry of announcing the Gospel in word and deed that was so intense that they sometimes "did not even have time to eat" (see Mk 6:31), to be intensively apprenticed to and formed by him, to be sent out by him to do the very deeds of teaching, healing, liberating, and enlivening that he did (see Lk 10:1–11; Mk 6:7–13), and after the resurrection to continue, full time, his lifestyle and ministry even unto the laying down of their lives (see Mt 28:16–20; Jn 21; Acts 1:78, 12–14 and elsewhere). We know the names of some members of this small itinerant group: Mary Magdalene, Simon Peter, Susanna, James and John—and later members like Paul and Barnabas who were assimilated to this group. This is the group, the form of discipleship, that supplies the primary biblical model for ministerial Religious Life.

I want to point out, from the New Testament, some of the characteristic features of this lifeform, which was learned by his disciples from Jesus himself and which they continued after his death and resurrection, so that we can discern more clearly the theological shape of ministerial Religious Life. I will deliberately contrast some of these features to those that are characteristic of other forms of discipleship in order to highlight the distinctiveness (not superiority) of this lifeform. Jesus did not propose this form of discipleship to all his followers, not even to some of his favorites like John the Baptist (called to desert hermit life) or Martha, Mary, and Lazarus (called to family life). He did not call to this form of life some of his most generous followers like the cured Gerasene demoniac (Lk 8:26–39) whom he sent back to his own people who would not allow Jesus himself to remain in their town. And some to whom Jesus proposed this itinerant form of discipleship, like the "rich young man," did not accept the invitation (see Mt 19:16–22). One, at least, accepted it but ended by betraying Jesus in an attempt to defeat his project.

It is crucial to recognize that there are diverse forms of discipleship, none of which is superior to any other (e.g., celibacy to family life, secular to religious, monastic to ministerial, lay to clerical). Only a mutually appreciative complementarity of and collaboration among disciples called to follow Jesus in a wide variety of ways will allow the Church to be and do what it must if the world God so loved is to be served and saved. But our purpose here is to look at Jesus' own personal lifestyle in which he formed this small itinerant band, which they continued to live after his departure and which is closely followed today by ministerial Religious.

Jesus began his ministerial life with prayer in solitude, a forty-day "retreat" in the desert during which he definitively renounced Satan and embraced his own God-given messianic vocation. But then he returned from the desert, in which he later occasionally sought prayerful solace, to a life of incredible ministerial exertion characterized by nearly incessant attention to the needs of the crowds who pressed upon him for food, healing, teaching, liberation from sin and even from death. Even when he attempted to take his itinerant band away to a secluded place "to rest awhile" the crowds followed him and he gave himself to them unstintingly because they were like "sheep without a shepherd" (see Mk 6:30–56).

Jesus participated actively and regularly in Sabbath liturgy (e.g., Mt 13:54; Mk 6:2; Lk 4:16; Jn 6:59) and went up to Jerusalem for the major feasts (e.g., Jn 2:13, 5:1, 10:22, 12:12). He was evidently knowledgeable in scripture, which he cited frequently and trenchantly, and the psalms came readily to his lips. But he also prayed, in joy and fear and agony, in words that were intimately his own, often spending whole nights or the pre-dawn hours in solitary prayer to the one he called his "Abba" (see Mk 1:35; Lk 6:12; Mt 14:23; Mk 6:46, and many other passages). Jesus celebrated with his disciples but also with other friends outside the itinerant band. He ate with religious officials and the wealthy but also with the poor, outcasts, and sinners, and even shared meals with those he knew were not well disposed toward him. He taught about God but most of his teaching was couched in secular terms, his parables being drawn from the daily life of homemakers and farmers and business people and parents and, though his words and saving acts were addressed primarily to his fellow Jews, they were not restricted to them (see Jn 4:46–54; Mt 15:21–28). In short, Jesus' personal choice was a mixed life of prayer, both communal and solitary, and intense ministerial action in the public sphere to Jews and non-Jews, to the religiously correct and those rejected by the religious officials, to women and men equally.

Jesus was an itinerant minister. He was not a member of a monastic community although there were such in the Judaism of his time and some scholars speculate that Jesus may have spent some time in one of them before embarking on his ministerial vocation. As he moved about to all the towns of Israel to which he had been sent (see Mk 1:38–39), he chose not to settle down, not to have a fixed abode, a home he could call his own and furnish according to his tastes and purposes. There was no place waiting for him at the end of the day, no stable much less enclosed community or routine of fixed prayers or activities on which he could rely for regularity, no prepared meals, no assured solitude or silence. Unlike the birds who have nests and foxes who have dens, he had nowhere to lay his head (see Mt 8:20). And those he called to share this life had to make the same choice: to leave behind home, gainful employment, stable work, possessions, family and friends and to share Jesus' life on the move (e.g., Mk 1:16–20; Mt 19:27–29). When he began sending them out on their own, to carry his mission forward, he made this itinerancy explicit: take no bag, no money, no extra clothes; make no provision for lodging; stay where you are invited and eat what you are served and demand no payment for your ministry (Lk 9:2–6 and par.). This was not a vocation for all or even for the majority; but for those called to it, it consisted in a close imitation of Jesus' own lifestyle.

Jesus and his itinerant band had no steady income since none of them was gainfully employed. In fact, Jesus called all of them to abandon their occupations and even divest themselves of accumulated personal property. They obviously lived a common economic life sharing a common purse (see Jn 13:29) and no one called anything his or her own. They seemed to receive support from followers and were invited into peoples' homes. But in any case, there is no evidence of total indigence on the one hand or of preoccupation about money, either making it or spending it, on the other. But they were clearly not a "for profit" enterprise.

Jesus was a celibate. By his own choice he made himself a "eunuch for the kingdom of God" (see Mt 19:10–12). He left his family of origin and resisted their attempts to lure (or even force) him back (see Mk 3:21). He did not marry (though he had close women friends), found a family (though he loved his own and participated in that of others), or have offspring (though he obviously loved children).

Jesus adopted no special clothing or other identifying markers. Unlike John the Baptist, Jesus did not dress like a prophet or an ascetic; unlike the hierarchy in Jerusalem he did not dress like a cleric or hierarch. He and his itinerant band never seemed to be disreputable or inappropriately attired when they were invited either to the homes of the poor or the banquet tables of the rich and no one in the Gospel ever remarks about their attire (though they do about Jesus' love of good dining! [Mt 11:19]). But Jesus had strong opinions about visible lifestyle characteristics among his followers. In Matthew 23:1–12 the historical Jesus is speaking to the scribes and Pharisees of his own lifetime and Matthew is addressing the Jewish authorities in his own context, but this passage is also aimed at Matthew's own Jewish-Christian community and its leaders. Jesus warns harshly against conspicuous religious apparel. Religious professionals are not to broaden their phylacteries or lengthen their tassels to make themselves stand out in public places so they will be greeted with deference and addressed with religious titles like rabbi, teacher, or father. They are not to pray or fast ostentatiously so as to be admired for their fervor (see Mt 6:5). They are not to take the front seats in the worshiping assembly or at public functions. Indeed he instructs them to seek inconspicuous places at public events (Lk 14:10) in solidarity with the poor and sinners.

Jesus was not prescribing how all disciples of all ages and cultures should live the external features of their lives. He was dealing with sincerity vs. hypocrisy, humility vs. pride, simplicity vs. ostentation. All disciples are called to personal and liturgical prayer, to the study of the scriptures, to service of their neighbors, to simplicity of lifestyle and humility in relationships, to inclusiveness and generosity. But Jesus himself did live a particular combination of particular expressions of all these characteristics and he did gather around himself a small band of women and men whom he initiated into this particular pattern of life. Down through the ages various groups have felt called to live that pattern, not just interiorly or in spirit but in concrete historical fact. Beginning with the original band of Jesus' itinerant disciples, through the consecrated virgins in the earliest Christian communities, the mendicants in the middle ages, the apostolic congregations of men and of women in the early modern period, down to the ministerial Religious of today, the Church has always had members who embraced this lifeform.

The salient features of this lifeform, deriving directly from that of the pre-Easter Jesus himself, include a total, lifelong consecration to God to the exclusion of any other primary life commitment (perpetual profession); the integration of a contemplative life of personal and shared prayer with a whole-hearted commitment to full-time public ministry in service of the Reign of God; community lived in mission (rather than in fixed abodes); a form of life that includes renunciation of family and home (consecrated celibacy), total personal economic dispossession and interdependence (evangelical poverty), ministry on a full-time basis (prophetic obedience in mission). However, such features as enclosed abode (cloister), special titles or culturally conspicuous dress (habit), fixed patterns of common vocal prayer, meals, and common manual labor (horarium) have sometimes been part of the life, especially when they were imposed on women by ecclesiastical authority, but are by no means intrinsic to or constitutive of the lifeform.

Anyone examining the life of ministerial women Religious in the United States today should have no difficulty recognizing their choice of and commitment to the pattern of life to which Jesus called his original band of itinerant disciples. Religious themselves are well aware of the difficulty of living in fidelity to this Gospel ideal in a contemporary first-world context. In a sex-saturated culture in which relationships are trivialized and infidelity seems ubiquitous, attracting women to lifelong consecrated celibacy and forming them to live it faithfully and fruitfully is a monumental challenge. Money plays a very different role in life today than it did in Jesus' time, and how to stay alive, support new and elderly members, and continue to minister freely as we have been commissioned by Jesus to do is a huge and unresolved problem, although much progress in this area has been made in the past four decades. Women Religious are, in general, deeply committed to the egalitarian, non-authoritarian, collegial exercise of authority and practice of obedience that Jesus inaugurated among his original band, but we live and minister in a Church that is not only rigidly hierarchical but functions as a divine right monarchy in which authority is functionally equated with coercive power and is entirely monopolized by men. Living situations in a first-world urban culture are not conducive to flexible and mobile community in mission nor supportive of shared spirituality. Liturgy is increasingly oppressive when it is not completely unavailable. Ecclesiastical support, financial or psychological, except from other Religious and the laity, is rare at best.

Despite these conditions, Religious know what they are called to, what they are trying to live. While it may not always be clear how to do it, most are quite clear that de-naturing their life is not the answer. Jesus never promised his disciples safety, approval, certitude, or comfort. He did promise that those who have left home, siblings, parents, children, lands for his sake and that of the Gospel will receive a hundredfold in this life, persecution, and finally eternal life (see Mk 10:29–30). Those who have persevered through the struggles of the conciliar renewal are sustained by a mysterious but real interior taste of that hundredfold. They certainly do not lack for persecution, especially at the present time! But they believe firmly in eternal life, possessed even now and awaiting them in all its fullness in "the age to come." For them, eternal life has a Name.

CHAPTER FOUR

RELIGIOUS LIFE AS PROPHETIC LIFEFORM IN THE CHURCH

INTRODUCTION

When the Vatican investigation of U.S. women Religious was announced some months ago without any preparation, consultation, or even the courtesy of a notification to congregational leaders that it was about to happen, many people, Religious and laity alike, were stunned at what seemed like a surprise attack aimed at a most unlikely target, given the massive and unaddressed problems besetting the clergy and hierarchy at the time. Persistent efforts to learn what the charges and who the accusers were hit a stone wall since virtually no one believed that a decline in numbers of entrants constituted a "crime" calling for such a massive response or that a juridical proceeding of such magnitude had been instituted to ascertain (much less foster!) the "quality of life" of Religious.

Little by little pressure from a variety of sources seems to have uncovered the answers to those two questions. The "charges" are that LCWR (Leadership Conference of Women Religious)–type congregations (that is, the vast majority of

Religious in the country) have implemented in their lives and in their ministries changes called for by Vatican II to the detriment (manifested in the decline in numbers of vocations) of Religious Life itself. Cardinal Rodé (the highest officer in Rome on Religious Life) believes, in his own words, that the Council precipitated the first "world-wide crisis" in the history of the Church and that women Religious, in his view, are primary promoters of that crisis in the United States.

The "accusers" are a small group of very traditionalist women Religious who, in September 2008, held a conference at Stonehill College in Massachusetts on consecrated life as they understand it, to which they invited Cardinal Rodé. At this conference, which included no presentation of positions at variance with their own, they put contemporary ministerial Religious Life on trial *in absentia*, found it seriously wanting, and raised the cry, "Investigate them!"

Cardinal Rodé, having heard what he apparently thought was a widely held consensus that U.S. women's apostolic Religious Life was in serious decline concluded, "We have no further need of witnesses." Unfortunately, he failed to consult the many thousands of Catholic laity who have received from women Religious their formation in the faith, ongoing spiritual support, pastoral care in times of need, and colleagueship in ministry, and who are now expressing their solidarity with the Sisters by petitions and personal letters of protest to the cardinal, the visitator, the Apostolic Delegate, and local ordinaries as well as by individual and collective testimonies to and about the Sisters (see, e.g., *U.S. Catholic,* "Entered into Evidence" [75:1, January 2010]). He failed to consult moderate bishops, like those in California, who have publicly testified that without women Religious their dioceses would not have become what they are and would not be functioning as well as they are today. He failed to consult significant groups of Religious outside the United

States, such as AMOR (conference of women Religious in Asia and Oceania) and UISG (International Union of Superiors General in Rome), which have expressed in public statements their appreciation of, support for, and solidarity with U.S. women Religious. He failed to consult the Sisters themselves who could have enlightened him on the small size and rigid ideological commitments of the one group of Religious he did consult and the few rightist bishops, in this country and in Rome, to whom he listened.

Many people, including many Religious, think this investigation is an unprecedented assault on Religious. Its scope may be unprecedented but its content certainly is not. Many, perhaps most, Religious congregations in this country have in their archives documents and correspondence chronicling equally or even more serious confrontations between their order and the local ecclesiastical authorities. (I suggest "Topic 11" in the excellent CD course, *The History of Women Religious in the United States*, by Margaret S. Thompson in the Now You Know Media Series, for archival documentation on this point.) These records, going back decades or even centuries, tell of threats and intimidation to enforce conscience-violating policies or practices (such as racial discrimination) instigated by members of the hierarchy, drastic sanctions for non-subordination to clergy in matters over which the clerics had no jurisdiction, demotion and even permanent exile without due process of lawfully elected and even revered superiors (including founders), appointment without election of compliant puppet governments, interference in appointments of Sisters, unilateral closing of institutions, forced acceptance of apostolates not appropriate to the congregation, and even outright theft of financial assets, to name only the most egregious examples.

Many Sisters, until very recently, did not know this part of their congregational histories. These often protracted and traumatic struggles were dark pages that, like many abuse victims, the corporate victims (the congregations) tried to bury or forget. Even when the abused know rationally that they are not to blame for what happened to them there is often a sense of deep shame, of being somehow responsible for inciting the abuse, of being "damaged goods" because of what one has undergone (especially if there is wide disparity of power and/or status between abuser and abused), of just wanting it to go away in hopes that it will never happen again.

Of course, it is still happening. The forced dispensation from vows of most of the members of the Los Angeles IHMs in the late 1960s by a furious Cardinal James F. McIntyre, who could not coerce these women to submit to his will; the years of struggle by superiors who refused to violate the consciences of the twenty-four women Religious who, in 1984, signed a *New York Times* statement asking for honest discussion (not a change of doctrine or even practice) of the issue of abortion that was seriously dividing the country and the Church; attempts, some successful and some not, to force the dismissal of Sisters legitimately appointed by their superiors to certain ministries, and so on, are within the memory of most Religious alive today. In other words, there is nothing new (except perhaps the comprehensive scope of the present investigation) in the struggle between some elements of the hierarchy and women Religious.

One of the most pernicious and characteristic aspects of these episodes is the pervasive appeal to a supposed obligation to "blind obedience to hierarchical authority" as the legitimation for clerical control, and even abuse, of women Religious. This neuralgic issue of the meaning of obedience is central to the current investigation, and it is important to realize that it is not new, not precipitated by late twentieth-century developments in American society or the post-conciliar Church, and not likely to be settled by heavy-handed exercises of coercive power. The issue goes back to the Gospel and the life of Jesus in his religious and social setting, and it will be clarified only by faithful meditation on the scriptures, prayer, and courageous action.

There is an instructive parallel between the questions Religious are asking about the Vatican investigation (and which they have asked before, many times, in similar situations) and the questions scholars (and many ordinary believers) ask about the trial and execution of Jesus. There is a tendency to ask, and to stop with, the questions "*Who* is responsible for the death of Jesus?" and "*Why* was Jesus executed?" (Like *who* is responsible for this investigation and *what* are the charges?)

At one level the answers are fairly easily available to a careful study of the Gospel texts. Jesus was executed *by* the collusion of the political (Roman Empire) and religious (Jerusalem hierarchy) power elites in first-century Palestine. He was executed *because* his ministry threatened to cause an uprising of the Palestinian peasantry. This would have been fatal to the career of Pontius Pilate, the Roman governor whose job was to keep the Jewish province under control. It would have been even more disastrous for the Jewish leadership who retained what little authority they had over their own religious affairs and population only as long as the Jewish populace did not become problematic for the Empire.

But this basically political-religious motivation is only a first-level answer to the questions of "who" and "why." It does not get at what we really need to know about Jesus and his mission if we want to understand the human predicament from which he came to save us and the radicality of the solution to that predicament that God offered us in Jesus. Until we realize that it is really the *human race*, including me/us, rather than a few historical figures in first-century Palestine, who crucified Jesus we do not yet "get it." Until we realize that the reason for his execution is *anthropological, theological, soteriological*, rather than merely regionally political or religious, and that those factors permeate the experience of the whole human race, we have not begun to plumb the real meaning of the paschal mystery or of our own implication in it.

Jesus' prophetic ministry of word and work was not merely a threat to the particular domination systems of Rome and Jerusalem. It was a fundamental subversion of domination itself as the demonic structure operative in human history. The incarnation was God's revelation in Jesus that God is not a Supreme Power controlling humanity through fear of damnation or extinction, nor the legitimator of human domination systems, but One who has chosen loving solidarity unto death with us to free us from all fear and bring us into the "liberty of the children of God."

Jesus was the end of all domination systems, all systems of salvation by the power exercised by a few over the many. No such system, political or religious, could ever again claim divine sanction. It was this definitive subversion of the violent human way of running the world by God's loving way of luring creation, including us, toward union with Godself that was the ultimate threat Jesus represented. The demonic "world," the kingdom of Satan, was undone by Jesus who was bringing into existence a new creation, an entirely different "world" which "God so loved as to give the only Son." In this new creation those who held power, Rome and Jerusalem, males and masters, strong and rich, were finished. This is why Jesus had to be killed. The historical reasons were real. But they were the local, even surface, manifestation of the deeper reason, which involved the re-orientation of the entirety of human history.

Analogously, it is not very complicated, or illuminating, to figure out that women's Religious Life is being used as a symbolic scapegoat in the power struggle in the contemporary Church between the promoters of the renewal initiated by Vatican II and a program of Tridentine restoration. Nor is it difficult to identify those who have vested interests in the outcome of that struggle. (This is not to suggest that the stakes in this struggle are not very high or that we should be naïve about the extent of damage that could result.) As Empire and Temple were threatened by the growing sense of empowerment among the oppressed in Palestine, so the absolutist power structure of the institutional Church is threatened by the growing consciousness of the People of God of their identity and mission as the Body of Christ. As Jesus was an agent of empowerment who had to be eliminated before he "stirred up the people" and brought down the wrath of the Empire on the nation, so those in the Church, lay leaders, pastors, bishops, or others—but especially Sisters—who are fostering the conciliar renewal must be brought under control lest the "crisis" Cardinal Rodé has named explode and bring about a radical claiming of their identity as the People of God and their mission to and in solidarity with the world God so loved.

But why the Sisters? We must not overlook the crushing of lay initiatives, the banning of progressive bishops from traditionalist bishops' dioceses, the brandishing of excommunications, the refusal of the sacraments or Christian burial, and public condemnations of Catholic politicians and theologians, and so forth as we examine the investigation of Religious. This is not a historically unique occurrence, and women Religious are not alone as its objects.

But Sisters are a particularly important target for several reasons. First, there is the matter of their sheer numbers and influence. Women Religious are not only people who are voluntarily engaged in the life they lead because they are passionately committed to its spiritual and ministerial goals and to Jesus Christ who called them to this life. They are also the largest, best organized, most geographically ubiquitous, most ministerially diversified, and therefore probably most effective promoters of the vision of Vatican II. In the eyes of some, of course, this means that, as so many lay Catholics have testified, Religious are the greatest source of hope for the contemporary Church. In the eyes of others, it means that they are the most serious danger to the "real (that is, pre-conciliar) Church," which these people are trying to restore.

Second, as relatively public figures in the Church, women Religious are easier to target. The (unsuccessful) attempt by the investigation to identify in writing every single individual woman Religious in the country by name, age, location, and ministry appeared decidedly more than a routine survey to anyone with eyes to see.

Third, the objects of this investigation are all women. Male Religious whose numbers have declined as steeply as women's are not under investigation even though, in its 1983 revision, Canon Law (§606) specified that women and men Religious should be treated equally unless some specific reason (not based on gender as such) made differential treatment necessary. The Roman Catholic Church is the most resolutely patriarchal organization in the Western world. Keeping women in absolute subjection to male authority is critical to the maintenance of patriarchy.

But, as in the question about the execution of Jesus, there is something much more important at stake for Religious in the question about the "why" and the "who" of this investigation, namely, the meaning of their life as a participation in the prophetic mission of Jesus rather than as a support system for an ecclesiastical power structure. What understanding of the theology and spirituality of ministerial Religious Life as a prophetic lifeform in the Church is in contention? What understanding of the critical role of Religious obedience in the exercise of that prophetic vocation is in dispute as this current drama unfolds? It is the biblical, historical, and theological examination of these deeper questions that I want to address in this chapter.

TRANSITION

In an article previously published by the *NCR* (chapter 3 of this book), I described ministerial Religious Life as it emerged in the Church in the 1500s, was officially approved in 1900, and has finally become distinct, in the wake of Vatican II, from the semi-cloistered monastic-apostolic hybrid lifeform of the early 1900s. I described it as a lifeform closely modeled on that of Jesus' original itinerant band of disciples, those women and men like Peter, Mary Magdalene, and others whom Jesus called to go about with him on a full-time basis in Palestine during his earthly ministry and, after his resurrection, to the ends of the earth. Like Jesus himself they were called to leave home, family, employment, personal belongings, and life projects and to devote themselves full time to the ministry of proclaiming the Reign of God in word and deed.

In this chapter I want to go beyond the description of the *itinerant lifestyle* of these disciples into the theological nature of the *prophetic lifeform* that this lifestyle embodies. In such an exploration of one lifeform in the Church we need always to keep in mind that all believers, whatever their particular Christian vocation, are equally called to discipleship and to holiness. However, not all disciples are called to this particular lifeform which, as we will see, consists in a particular assimilation to Jesus' prophetic identity and mission.

John Paul II insisted at considerable length in *Vita Consecrata* (the post-synodal apostolic exhortation published in 1996, Part II, 84 ff.), following the lead of the Council, that Religious Life is a *prophetic* lifeform in the Church. Prophecy is not all there is to Religious Life, just as it did not exhaust the mission and ministry of Jesus. But our question here is, what does it mean to say that ministerial Religious Life is essentially a prophetic lifeform? Only from this basis can we address

some of the questions about the life, and particularly about
the role of obedience in this life, that are being raised by the
current Vatican investigations.

THE PRE-PASCHAL JESUS AS PROPHET:
MODEL OF RELIGIOUS LIFE

The Fact

Throughout his public ministry Jesus functioned as a prophet
recognizably in the tradition of the Old Testament prophets,
especially Moses, Elijah, Isaiah, Jeremiah, Ezekiel, and Hosea
who are evoked explicitly and implicitly in the narrative of
Jesus' life, death, and resurrection. People clearly regarded
Jesus as a prophet (see Mt 14:5, 21:11, 21:46; Lk 7:16, 7:39; Jn
6:14), and he did not reject or refuse this identification as he
did that of king. On the contrary, Jesus spoke of himself as a
prophet by comparing himself to the prophet Jonah (see Mt
12:39), identifying himself as the prophet not accepted in his
own town or among his own people (see Lk 4:24), and predicting that he would suffer the fate of the prophets, namely,
persecution by the religious authorities and finally execution
in the Holy City (see Lk 13:33).

In John's Gospel there are two extraordinary scenes in
which the pre-Easter Jesus' prophetic identity is progressively
discerned by his textual interlocutors and clearly revealed to
the readers. In John 4 the Samaritan woman starts by seeing
Jesus as a "man" and a "Jew," and then recognizes that he is
a "patriarch" greater than Jacob, and finally exclaims, "I per-
ceive that you are a prophet" (Jn 4:19). In John 9 the healed
man-born-blind starts by referring to his healer as "the man
called Jesus" and goes on to solemnly testify before the Jewish authorities (at the cost of excommunication) that Jesus
"is a prophet" (Jn 9:17) come from God.

After the Resurrection, when the risen Jesus, unrecognized, joins the two disciples on the way to Emmaus and asks them what they are discussing as they walk, they reply that they are talking about "Jesus of Nazareth, a prophet mighty in word and work before God and all the people" (Lk 24:19) and whom their leaders have executed. Obviously, they are voicing the perception of Jesus' identity common among his followers.

The itinerant band of followers who accompanied Jesus during his public life and were commissioned by him after his Resurrection to continue his mission were initiated into Jesus' own prophetic ministry by Jesus himself. Many ministries of the word, such as apostleship, evangelization, and teaching developed in the early Church and there was much overlapping among them. All of them had a prophetic dimension though each was specified by distinctive goals such as proclaiming the Gospel to people who had not yet heard it or catechizing converts. Religious Life, as the lifeform most closely modeled on that of Jesus' original itinerant band, also involves participation in these various forms of ministry of the word. But I want to suggest that one of those ministries, prophecy, is central to and defining of the Religious lifeform as it was of Jesus' pre-Easter ministerial life.

Since I am interested here in the essentially prophetic character of ministerial Religious Life I will not attempt a comprehensive phenomenology or theology of prophecy in general. (I suggest the still inspiring work of Abraham Heschel, *The Prophets* [1962] as a resource for understanding Old Testament prophecy and Marcus Borg's *Jesus* [2006], especially chapters 7–10, on Jesus as prophet, as well as Walter Brueggemann's *The Prophetic Imagination* [rev. ed., 2001] on the spirituality of prophecy). Rather, I will examine the life of Jesus as prophet under three headings in order to show, in the next section, the parallel between Jesus' prophetic vocation and Religious Life as a prophetic lifeform in the Church. I will look at Jesus' mission and ministry in terms of his prophetic *call*, his *task* as prophet, and his *life* as prophet.

The Prophet's Call

The first thing to say about biblical prophecy is that it is *not about foretelling the future*, predicting what will happen at a chronologically later date. Prophecy is *about telling the absolute future of God*, what Jesus called "The Reign of God," *into the present*. The prophet is immersed in the life of the people in a particular place and time and is commissioned by God to interpret that situation in the light of God's dream for this people and the whole of humanity. Listening to the voice of God, reading the "signs of the times" (see Mt 16:13), and focusing the word of God in the present is the defining feature of prophecy.

In Israel's history, for example, Moses was called by God in his inaugural experience at the burning bush and commissioned by God to interpret the experience of the Hebrew people in the light of God's plan for them: liberation, desert journey, covenant, entrance into and life in the Promised Land within their global vocation to be a "light to the nations." Jesus was sent by God, as a first-century Palestinian Jew among Jews, to interpret their experience of oppression under the colluding domination systems of the Roman Empire and the Jerusalem Temple in light of God's plan for them, a plan for *shalom*, universal well-being and flourishing as the People of God.

The prophet is not a divine "ambassador pleni-potentiary" from God, someone who alone has independent or absolute access to God's plan. The prophet is *part of the people* to whom he or she is sent, nurtured from birth in the religious and social wisdom of that people, product of its history, participant in its prayer, inheritor of its dreams, victim of and sometimes even sharer in its sins and errors. It is because the prophet is one with the people that he or she can speak for this people to God and for God to this people.

But the prophet, one of and with the people, is also in a *special relationship with God.* Most of the great prophetic figures, like Moses, Jeremiah and Hosea, Mary, and Jesus himself were called by God to their special mission in some kind of intense, transformative, revelatory religious experience that scripture presents as an "inaugural vision" or a prophetic call. Jesus' baptism followed by the desert temptations are presented as such an experience. God takes possession of the prophet in a special way, more or less to the exclusion of any other major life commitment, and forms the prophet spiritually—Marcus Borg says "mystically" in Jesus' case—to mediate the special interaction between God, this people, and the particular historical situation.

However, the prophet is not a puppet. Everything depends on the prophet's obedience, the prophet's "yes." Jesus' "Be gone, Satan" and choice to serve God alone (Mt 4:10) in response to God's choice of him as "Beloved Son," or Mary's "Be it done to me according to [God's] word" (Lk 1:36) in response to her call to be mother of the messiah, exemplify the partnership of God and the prophets in the great work to which God calls them.

Luke underlines the continuity between Jesus and his prophetic forebears by constructing a dramatic scene of Jesus' emergence into public ministry. Jesus, in the synagogue of his home town, quotes Isaiah in reference to himself to express his self-understanding of his mission:

> When he came to Nazareth, where he had been brought up, he went to the synagogue on the Sabbath day, as was his custom. He stood up to read, and the scroll of the prophet Isaiah was given to him. He unrolled the scroll and found the place where it was written:

"The Spirit of the Lord is upon me, because he has anointed me to bring good news to the poor. He has sent me to proclaim release to the captives and recovery of sight to the blind, to let the oppressed go free, to proclaim the year of the Lord's favor." ... Then he began to say to them, "Today this scripture has been fulfilled in your hearing." (Lk 4:16–21)

It is not surprising that many ministerial Religious congregations refer to this passage in their Constitutions or supplementary literature. Religious recognize this description of Jesus the prophet as their own ministerial *magna carta*.

Finally, the prophet's mission takes place in and is directed to *a particular historical situation*. This helps account for the ambiguity of the prophet's mission, which is always open to more than one interpretation, at least by the community and its neighbors, if not, often enough, by the prophet him or herself. Prophetic speaking and acting do not have the advantage of hindsight precisely because they are addressed to "what is happening" right now.

This is the cause of one of the major points of contention between ministerial Religious and some ecclesiastical officials today as well as in the past. Are Religious a general ecclesiastical "work force" to be deployed by the hierarchy according to institutional needs, or are they called to respond to particular, actual challenges in a variety of particular places and settings among particular groups and people of all kinds (some of whom are rejected by the religious institution itself) whose needs cry out for ministerial attention? The theology of "charism" in relation to Religious Life itself and the variety of congregations, as we will see, suggests the latter. If this is the case, Religious are, by vocation, much less "controllable," less predictable, and readily submissive than some officials would like.

The Prophet's Task

The task of the prophet is to bear witness to God, by word and work, to God's people in a particular context or historical situation. Let us look first at the *word and work* of Jesus within which God and the new dispensation that God is inaugurating in Israel emerge into clarity.

Because prophecy is concrete and particular rather than abstract and general the prophet tends to use a *particular "genre" or type of speech.* The pre-Easter Jesus (more accurately pictured by the synoptics than by John in this regard) did not usually teach formally in the sense of expounding scriptural texts or official ecclesiastical positions, giving long theological or moral discourses, or explaining difficult concepts. His discourse was metaphorical and participative.

First, the prophet's message is not about "the world beyond" or outside this one. Jesus tended to teach metaphorically, by parable ("likeness" stories) or aphorism (pithy "one-liners"). His stories and aphorisms were about everyday realities in this world: about farming and baking, shepherding or tax collecting; about parents and children, guests and strangers, traveling and building, borrowing and lending, marrying, giving birth, dying. They functioned to subvert the conventional wisdom associated with these everyday realities and thereby shed new light on the more important realities that they symbolized.

Second, Jesus' prophetic discourse was not simply expository. He often taught participatively, explicitly or implicitly asking his hearers, "What do you think?" Who showed himself neighbor to the one who fell among robbers? Would you, if you were the older son, go into the celebration for your renegade brother? Was the father of the prodigal a naïve chump or a God figure? Which is the greatest commandment? What would that vineyard owner do to those wicked tenants? Would you have stoned her? Should the last shift workers have gotten as much as the first shift ones? The question, inviting the hearer to moral responsibility, rather than the prescribed answer, is characteristic of prophetic engagement.

The other major device of the prophets, besides their particular metaphorical and participative rhetoric, was their works, their *symbolic actions*, sometimes explained and sometimes left for the viewer to interpret. Jesus revealed God through acts of healing, exorcism, and other works of power. But one of Jesus' most striking symbolic actions, repeated again and again in numerous settings and expressing the new dispensation God was establishing, was crossing social and religious boundaries, subverting the purity rules of Israel.

Jesus did this in myriad ways but the most striking was his open table fellowship. A major charge against Jesus was, "He welcomes sinners and tax-collectors and eats with them" (Lk 15:2). He also touched or let himself be touched by "unclean" people like lepers (see Mk 1:41), or a hemorrhaging woman (Mt 9:20), or a corpse (Lk 7:14). He ate with unpurified hands out of unkosher dishes (see Mk 7:2–20). He let sinners touch him, intimately (see Lk 7:39). He interacted with women in public and private without the presence of male family members (see Jn 4). He spoke with, learned from, and even marveled at the faith of non-Jews (e.g., Mt 15:22–28; Lk 7:1–9).

Lest we think the Jews were finicky legalists completely unlike our own religious selves, we might want to consider some of our own rules and regulations. Who are the "sinners" we excommunicate or exclude from our sacramental table, the "unclean" we regard as "intrinsically disordered," the religious "others" whose faith we regard as "gravely defective"?

Finally, Jesus did highly provocative symbolic acts. He broke the sabbath for the sake of people in need (e.g., Mk 3:1–6). He even drove licensed functionaries out of the temple during a major feast, an unmistakably anti-temple act

(Mt 21:12–14). And he meekly rode a donkey into the Holy City through one gate just as the Emperor's representative, Pilate, was riding into it in royal splendor through the opposite gate, a deliberately anti-imperial gesture (see Mk 11:1–10; Mt 21:1–10). Such prophetic actions could hardly be taken lightly.

But what is this prophetic speaking and acting all about? *To what, or better to whom, was Jesus bearing witness?* Marcus Borg (*Jesus*, ch. 7) captures this well in two words: to God as *compassion*, and to *justice* as God's dream for humanity. Jesus, as we will discuss below, was a mystic or a contemplative, a man in deep experiential communion with God. God, for Jesus, was not an object of theological belief, much less a moral enforcer presiding over humanity from "heaven." The God Jesus had come to know intimately was not like the God in which many of his contemporaries, including many of the religious authorities, believed. Jesus' God is also not like the God in which many Christians, especially the self-righteous guardians of public morality we all can be at times, believe.

The God of Jesus was not only compassionate but *compassion itself*. In God there was no wrath, no violence, no vengeance or retaliation. Jesus' God drew no boundaries between those on the inside and those on the outside, the good sheep and the lost, the sinners and the upright, the clean and the unclean (except perhaps that Jesus seemed to prefer the less acceptable!). God had no purity requirements. The God of Jesus sent rain and sun on just and unjust alike (see Mt 5:45). Jesus' Abba was the parent of the prodigal, a God who was inconceivable in a legalistic framework where good and evil were rigorously defined and rewards and punishments stringently applied. The infinite compassion of God filled the heart of Jesus and poured out of him in his practice of total inclusivity and boundless free forgiveness.

Probably the most stunning story in the Gospel expressing this God-image of Jesus is not a parable but a narrated event. It is "housed" now in John's Gospel (Jn 7:53–8:11) where it obviously does not "belong." This text, often titled "A Woman Taken in Adultery," was an orphan text that appeared at various times in the history of the transmission of the New Testament in different gospels and in different places in the gospels. It has been hypothesized, not implausibly, that its checkered textual career testifies to the fact that it was too shocking to Church officials to be easily admitted as scripture and too cherished by the people to be successfully suppressed. It was finally included in the Catholic canon but it remains a not easily domesticated narrative.

The religious officials drag before Jesus a woman taken in the very act of adultery. She is, without doubt, guilty of breaking one of the most serious commandments of the Law. Adultery is a capital offense (see Dt 22:23–24), and the scribes and Pharisees (the clerical caste and spiritual elite) test Jesus by asking him what he has to say about the stoning prescribed by the Law of Moses. "Are you for it or against it?" If you say to stone her, you agree that God is as we represent him, a just but harsh judge who is unrelenting toward sinners (not the wishy-washy parent of the prodigal that Jesus had been preaching!). If you oppose her execution, you oppose the Law of Moses (and thereby prove that you do not come from God or speak for God). Or, at least, you oppose our administering the Law, thereby showing that you accept Rome's denial to the Jews of the power to execute (which proves your allegiance is to the Empire rather than to God). The three-way trap is set with this woman as bait.

Jesus does not enter into an argument about the nature of God or sexual morality, about the validity of the Law or about the authority of the hierarchy, or even about the reach of Roman jurisdiction. He simply turns the focus from the woman to the religious officials themselves. He does not say adultery is all right. He does not say the woman is innocent.

He does not dispute the legitimacy of capital punishment. He does not ask where her accomplice is or who was eyewitness to the offense. He does not even ask if she is repentant. He says in effect, "The case may be exactly as you say. The problem is, where can we find someone who is qualified to apply the penalty? Is there one among you who is sinless and is therefore qualified to punish a sinner?"

When they all quietly disappear the woman is left facing the one person who is indeed qualified to execute her, the one person who is without sin. But he refuses to enter into the dynamics of the case. He just asks, "Has no one condemned you?" Obviously, the answer is "No." Then, he says, "Neither do I."

If the one who is qualified to condemn simply declines to do so, what becomes of dominant power, of condemnation and punishment, as a way of handling evil and maintaining moral order? The enormity of this question is quite probably the reason this text had trouble getting into the canon. What would happen to good order in society or the Church if this suspension of condemnation became common practice? Jesus tells the woman to "sin no more," indicating that he knows and names as sin what she has done. He is not declaring a moral free-for-all among humans. But he also, shockingly, does not indicate that this woman is a one-time exception, a useful pedagogical tool but the only person God will ever treat this way.

Jesus' symbolic act seems to say something about God that is inconceivable, and totally unacceptable, in a framework of law, sin, judgment, retribution, punishment—in the human program of how to run a tight moral ship in a religious institution. He seems to be suggesting by this prophetic act, as he did with the parable of the Prodigal Son, that God is operating in a framework that is radically different from ours, one that makes no appeal to coercive power.

Indeed, he seems to be saying that *God* is radically different from us and that our image of God says more about *us* than about God.

If God's nature is boundless compassion, total inclusivity, absolute free forgiveness, what does this imply for us? Borg says that if *compassion* is God's nature then *justice* is God's passion. Justice, however, is not divine retribution carried out by humans but right relations among humans who are all equally sinners and between humans who are all sinful and God who is infinite compassion. Justice is not "an eye for an eye" but the definitive eradication of all that is contrary to compassion, namely, anger, violence, vengeance, oppression, domination, and all their kin. Many of Jesus' parables and sayings bear directly on the issues of justice such as the equitable distribution of material necessities, generosity, peaceful reconciliation of differences, non-violence, inclusiveness, forgiveness of enemies, the equality of persons including women, children, the lower class, slaves, the poor and the sick, and even foreigners. In other words, justice is compassion in action.

Jesus the prophet was not preaching generalities about God or God's desire for the people. As a prophet he was addressing a very particular historico-religious situation. He was preaching an alternate reality from that of first-century official Judaism under Roman occupation. Jesus was describing, "parabling" into the imagination of his hearers, a new "world." He called it the "Kingdom of God."

While many contemporary Christians prefer "reign of God" because it is less patriarchal than "kingdom," Jesus used "kingdom" for a reason. By calling the reality he had been sent to inaugurate a kingdom—since there could not be two different kingdoms in operation in the same place at the same time—he was invalidating the violent imperium of the Romans. He was inviting his hearers to live in a new kingdom structured by inclusive, compassionate love and justice, a kingdom in which only God is sovereign. Such a kingdom is indeed a reign, but not a domination system, not a two-tiered world in which a small minority controls almost all resources, economic and political, while the vast majority teeter on the edge of destitution.

But it was not only Roman imperial rule, the economic and political domination system of the Empire, that Jesus was calling into question. By presenting a socio-religious order that was radically different from that supported by the Temple authorities he was also calling *that* regime, the religious domination system, into question. By his inclusivity, his transgressing of purity boundaries, his reimagining of sin and forgiveness, he was dismantling a kind of carefully structured religious world based on law and inaugurating a new way of relating to God with implications for a new way of relating to one another.

Jesus' Sermon on the Mount, with his resounding prophetic, "but I say to you," interiorized the Law without invalidating its external observance. His symbolic action in the temple interiorized worship without declaring public worship invalid. But, when all was said and done, there remained only the double law of total love of God and total love of neighbor. For Jesus this was "the whole law and the prophets" (see Mt 22:35–40). Anything that could not fit under that rubric was peripheral and relative and could be put aside if necessary to further the agenda of love.

We know well that Jesus, like the prophets of Israel before him, did not "succeed" in his prophetic mission. He suffered the fate of the prophet that he himself had described (see Mt 23:29–36). He died as the victim of the Empire in collusion with the Temple authorities. If the story had ended there we would have proof that his prophetic mission was a fool's errand rather than a divine commission, a quixotic dream that could not come true in the "real world" where evil can be handled only by force. But the story did not end there. God raised Jesus from the dead and Jesus committed his prophetic mission to his followers.

In summary, Jesus is the embodiment of the prophetic mission and his ministry is the expression in action, in word and work, of that mission. His mission was to "tell into the present," by word and deed, the absolute future of God which is what the synoptics call the "Reign of God," John calls "eternal life," and Paul usually calls "life in the Spirit." That reality is a new dispensation in which all are called to share, here and now. It is the dispensation of *shalom*, which is the earthly realization of the love of God in the community of love of neighbor. It is God's compassion expressed in human justice. This, not institutional or ecclesiastical projects, and certainly not a religious domination system, is what Religious are called to serve. Jesus, in prophetic word and work, not in institution maintenance, is the model of ministry for Religious.

The Prophet's Life

We turn finally to Jesus' life out of which his prophetic ministry flowed. Is it a realistic model for the life of ministerial Religious today? If so, what are the implications of the prophetic character of Religious Life for the behavior of Religious in ministry and in relation to the hierarchy?

First, Jesus' prophetic vocation was rooted in and expressive of his *mystical life*, the intense contemplative prayer life that the gospels present as the root of his *experiential knowledge of God*. He not only took part in Jewish vocal prayer and liturgy (e.g., see Lk 4:16; Mt 26:17). He also spent long periods—whole nights (Lk 6:12), hours before dawn (Mk 1:35), times of decision making (Lk 6:12–13) and anguish (see Mk 14:32–42), and, at least once, "forty days"—in prayer to God (see Mk 1:13 and pars.). Jesus not only knew about God; he *knew God* intimately. He experienced God as his "Abba" (Mk

14:36), his loving parent, from whom he drew his own identity, and whose project was his own. In John's Gospel Jesus speaks of being "one" with God (Jn 10:30) whose words he speaks and whose works he does (see Jn 14:10). The prophet's direct and immediate experience of God is the root of her or his words and actions. But this activity is often enough critical of or even in opposition to the positions of the legitimate ecclesiastical authorities who are usually presented as, and in fact are, God's institutional representatives. Jesus' confrontation with the officials over the woman taken in adultery was not an isolated case. He was frequently in heated conflict with the hierarchy.

We can be tempted to think that such opposition to institutional authority was fine for Jesus in relation to the Jerusalem hierarchy in the first century but not for us in relation to ecclesiastical authority in our own time. Jesus, after all, was God, so he knew all the right answers. And the Jerusalem hierarchy were degenerate and evil hypocrites.

To sanitize (and even trivialize) Jesus' prophetic ministry in this way is to miss the point entirely. Jesus did not claim personal divine authority when he acted prophetically in relation to the religious institution. He claimed to be speaking *for* God, not *as* God. And it is important to note that his adversaries were claiming exactly the same thing, that is, to be God's official representatives to the people which, in fact, they were. They actually had the ecclesiastical authority of office on their side, which Jesus did not because he was not a priest, an elder, a scribe, or any other kind of religious official.

Jesus had prophetic credibility among the people because he "spoke with authority," precisely *not as the scribes*, that is, not by virtue of institutional position nor backed up by texts (see Mk 1:27; Mt 7:29). He spoke "like no other person ever has" (cf. Jn 7:45–46). It was not because he was God in thin disguise or because he was credentialed by the religious establishment, but because his truth telling, despite over-whelming personal threat when what he said and did ran counter to what the laws or the officials required, manifested to the people that he was indeed representing the true God. Only later, only after the Resurrection, did they realize that this "prophet, mighty in word and work," was indeed the Son of God. During his public life, his authority flowed from what he did and said. No one can confer, and no one can "claim," moral authority. It belongs only to one who earns it by the integrity of their life, the coherence between what they say and what they live. Jesus was powerfully, personally authoritative and that is why he was recognized as a prophet.

Furthermore, the religious officials of Jesus' time were no more wicked, hypocritical, oppressive, immoral, or corrupt than officials of state and Church in other ages. They had the same status among their contemporaries as do our legislators, priests and bishops, presidents, and popes. The presumption of legitimacy and competence was theirs by virtue of their office. The officials Jesus confronted were not wearing signs saying embezzler, hypocrite, pedophile, adulterer, pornographer, so that anyone looking at them would know that Jesus was certainly right to call them to account. Jesus was seeing in them, in their teaching and their behavior, what his contemporaries, like so many of us when we deal with people in high places, were conditioned *not* to see, or were *afraid* to name. And he bore witness, at the risk of his life, to what he saw.

The problem for Jesus' contemporaries was the same as ours today. How are we to judge between voices competing for our acceptance? How do we recognize the prophet, the one who "speaks for God"? Obviously, as the horror of the Holocaust made clear for all time, it is profoundly immoral to uncritically "follow orders" simply because they come from someone in authority. Jesus warned his contemporaries to beware of the official teachers, of the priests and elders and Pharisees who "sit in the chair of Moses" but are hypocrites (see Mt 23:2–3), whited sepulchers (see Mt 23:27), self-serving oppressors of the poor in the name of God.

There were, of course, sincere men among the ecclesiastical officials of Jesus' time, like the Pharisee Nicodemus (Jn 3, 7, 19) and the scribe who was "not far from the kingdom of God" (Mk 12:28–39). But there were many others, like Caiaphas (Jn 11:49–50 with 18:14), who were "the blind leading the blind" (see Mt 15:10–14). We face the same challenge today. There are many men of integrity, holiness, and compassion holding office in the Church. But popes can be wrong, even culpably so; bishops can be criminals; priests can be embezzlers or sexual predators. One thing is certain: hierarchical status, office in the Church, is no guarantee that the speaker or his message comes from God. An office holder may be prophetic, or a prophet may hold office, but the two charisms as such do not imply each other. And history suggests that there is virtually always tension, if not opposition, between institutional and prophetic authority.

Besides an intense life of prayer that unites the prophet to God, a second requirement of prophetic identity and mission is a certain *freedom from attachments* that pressure the person to prefer personal or institutional goods, the maintaining of the *status quo* within which one's own position and interests are protected, to God's interests or the good of those to whom one is sent. Jesus was extraordinarily "unattached" not only inwardly, but even in his personal lifestyle. By his own choice, he had no family to provide for or to protect. He owned no personal property that he could lose. He held no official position of power, political or ecclesiastical, that his actions could jeopardize.

Of course, family, property, and power are not necessarily impediments to prophetic freedom. Like St. Thomas More, many people in high places, with much to protect personally, professionally, and politically, have given their lives in witness to the truth. But being without such attachments is a bulwark of prophetic freedom simply because it makes it easier to "hear," without distortion from one's own inner voices or outer demands, the voices that are relevant to the issues one must discern. With less "static" from legitimate competing interests the prophet can more easily listen full time, with all his or her attention, for the truth to which witness is required, the truth that must be done regardless of orders to the contrary. Discernment based on attentive listening, not submission to the will of another, is the essence of prophetic obedience.

Third, a major and non-negotiable criterion of the true prophet is the *coherence between the prophet's message and the prophet's life.* The more insensitive one is to the devastation one's teaching or legislating causes in the lives of real people, the more willing one is to "stone the sinner" in order to bolster official authority and guard public morality, the more likely it is that, no matter how highly placed, one is a "blind guide," one of those Jesus described who "tie up heavy burdens, hard to bear, and lay them on the shoulders of others; while they themselves are unwilling to lift a finger to move them" (Mt 23:4). Rosa Parks and Nelson Mandela were willing to pay the price for their witness for racial justice. Jesus defending the woman taken in adultery was risking his life for hers. Witness to the truth is never comfortable or self-aggrandizing for the true prophet, and the risks are usually high. "Witness" from the favored side of power is dubiously prophetic.

The issue that emerges as central when the prophetic charism conflicts with institutional authority is precisely the one operative in much of the current struggle between the institutional Church and Religious, namely, obedience. Can we equate obedience to God with doing what we are told by people who hold office? And can we submissively abstain from interpreting the present situation in light of the Gospel and responding to the present needs of real people because those who hold office require that we do so?

We will return to this topic shortly, but, by way of anticipation, it appears from Jesus' practice and especially from his life that religious obedience cannot be adequately understood or defined as "blind or absolute submission to official authority," whether to people, teaching, or laws. No matter how highly placed in the religious institution they might be, human beings do not take God's place in the life of believers. To pretend otherwise is blasphemy on the part of those who claim to do so and idolatry on the part of those who accord to humans the obedience that belongs to God alone. There is no avoiding the challenge and the obligation of discernment, and "blind obedience," that is, uncritical submission to power, is neither discernment nor obedience—nor can it ever be a substitute for either.

Coming to grips, in genuine obedience to God, with the tension between their prophetic vocation and the demands of ecclesiastical authority is at the heart of the current struggle between Religious and the Vatican. So we turn now to a focused examination of contemporary ministerial Religious Life against the background of the understanding of Jesus' prophetic vocation in which Religious are called to share.

RELIGIOUS LIFE AS A PROPHETIC LIFEFORM

Crucial Distinctions

Religious Life has been called a prophetic lifeform both in official documents and in spiritual writings almost since its inception. The meaning of this affirmation, however, is often unrealistically romanticized or left so piously vague as to be useless. In the current situation in which the nature of ministerial Religious Life as a prophetic lifeform in the Church is in public contention it would be helpful for us, as a Church in general and as Religious in particular, to clarify the meaning of this affirmation.

First, it is the *lifeform*, not the individual Religious, that is characterized as "prophetic." Just as entrance into an enclosed monastic community (often called a "contemplative order") does not make one a contemplative, and there are many genuine contemplatives who do not enter monasteries, so entering Religious Life does not make one a prophet and there are many prophetic figures who do not enter Religious Life. However, different lifeforms in the Church offer corporate witness (corporate as in "organic," not as in "corporation") to particular dimensions of Christian life in which all the baptized are called to participate. All are called to contemplation, to fidelity and fruitfulness, to prophetic witness. But certain lifeforms, such as enclosed monastic life, matrimony, or ministerial Religious Life raise one or another of these dimensions to particular visibility by their corporate living of this charism. So what follows makes no claims that all ministerial Religious are prophets or that Religious Life has any monopoly on the charism of prophecy in the Church.

However, the lifeform as *corporate witness to the charism of prophecy* does (or should) explicitly challenge its individual members to the exercise of this charism and empower, support, and promote their fidelity to this charism. The felt call to prophetic ministry and the gifts of spirit, mind, and heart for the exercise of such ministry, therefore, should be factors in discerning a vocation to Religious Life.

At certain times in its history, Religious Life has been so caught up in a hyper-institutionalized and over-clericalized understanding of Church and ministry, and of itself in that framework, that many congregations lost sight of this vocational criterion. They preferred candidates who were compliant and docile. The less experienced and competent, the more girlishly romantic about their calling, that they were at entrance, the better, since they were more easily "formed" for submission. Most congregations today prefer candidates who have a sturdy sense of self, developed through education and work experience, and sufficient maturity to live and work well outside a "total institution" environment. Such candidates are more likely to grow into a truly prophetic ministerial identity and spirituality.

Second, some can be tempted to label "prophetic" any kind of protest that is extreme, conspicuous, or stubborn, or to claim the title of "prophet" for anyone whose ideas or behavior are questioned by authority, no matter how reasonably. The truly prophetic are typically very reluctant to call themselves prophets. They know well their fear in the face of conflict and the high cost of putting themselves in the line of fire of angry officials. Furthermore, they recognize the need to receive seriously and incorporate responsibly institutional authority's positions and concerns into any discernment that influences other people, in or outside the Church. Again, discerning between the genuinely prophetic stance and mob fanaticism, between courage and arrogance can be very difficult. It requires prayer, communal consultation, testing, and a humble willingness to consider seriously all reasonable and respectful disagreement with one's position.

The Inaugural Vision or Prophetic Call

Religious Life begins, both corporately and individually, in an experience analogous to the inaugural vision of the Old Testament prophets and of Jesus himself. Although the literary form of the biblical narratives of prophetic calls convey the substance but not necessarily the historical details of these experiences, all these texts indicate that the prophetic vocation is not undertaken on one's own initiative. Nor is one appointed to it by human beings. *The call comes from God,* often to one who feels frightened, unworthy, or incompetent. Even Jesus is clearly sobered by the dimensions and evident dangers of the life to which he is called. God's call to him is powerful and compelling, but Satan's opposition is both real and dangerous.

Religious orders begin, typically, in the charismatic experience of one or more founders who feel impelled to give themselves to God and God's work, almost always in response to some historically pressing need. Subsequent members respond to a personal call to join the founders in this divinely originated enterprise. The ensuing process of mutual discernment for later candidates is designed to test the "fit" between the prospective member, the foundational charism, and the historical shape that the order has taken since its founding.

Religious orders, then, are not the creations of the ecclesiastical institution (although it makes certain regulatory provisions regarding the living of the life, approves rules, and exercises some supervisory or protective functions in regard to approved institutes [*Lumen Gentium* VI, 45]), any more than the Old Testament prophets were appointed by Israel's kings or priests or Jesus by the Temple officials. In fact, those who functioned as "court prophets," who "worked for" the king or priests by telling them what they wanted to hear or leading the people to submit to their rulers when God spoke differently through the true prophets or "the signs of the times," were quintessentially "false prophets."

Religious Life, then, is a charismatic lifeform, called into existence by the Holy Spirit, to live corporately the prophetic charism in the Church. It is not a workforce gathering recruits for ecclesiastical projects and it does not receive its mission nor the particular ministries of its members from the hierarchy. Congregations, in the exercise of particular ministries within dioceses or parishes, are bound by the applicable local directives and must work collaboratively with the ordained leadership. But this does not put the congregation or its members "under" the bishop or clergy. This is especially true of "exempt" congregations that minister across ecclesiastical boundaries.

When members of the hierarchy get panicky about the decline in numbers of Religious they reveal a serious misunderstanding of the nature of the life. No congregation "needs" more members than are actually called to it by God. There is no optimal or minimum size for orders or length of their lifespan. Some orders have never had more than a few dozen members and others have thousands. Some are centuries old and others have had a very brief history. The purpose of the life is not to perpetuate particular congregations nor to staff Church institutions; it is to live intensely the witness to the Gospel to which the congregation is called and for as long as it is so called. As long as an order and its members are able to live Religious Life according to its own founding charism and approved constitutions, intrusion by ecclesiastical authority into its internal affairs is not only unwarranted, it is unjustifiable and counter-productive (see e.g., canon 586).

The Prophetic Task

As we have already seen, the distinguishing mark of the prophetic vocation among the various ministries of the word in the Church (e.g., apostleship, evangelization, preaching, teaching, etc.) is its task of focusing the word, the proclamation of the Reign of God, directly on and in *a particular situation*. Prophetic witness involves discerning and responding to what the Council, following Jesus, called "the signs of the times" (Mt 16:3). So, the prophet is not simply announcing the Gospel in general or explaining doctrines in the abstract.

This is why, historically, most orders speak of being "founded for" a particular ministry such as education or helping the poor. They are not actually founded to do a particular work such as "to teach in parochial schools." One does not have to become a Religious in order to be a Catholic-school teacher or social worker. But a particular situation demanding the proclamation of the Reign of God here and now gave rise to a question like, "What does the Gospel of the Reign of God mean, call for, demand, need in this situation of desperate ignorance or widespread poverty?"

Over time this charism of bearing prophetic witness in the sphere of education, for example, may evolve into addressing all kinds of ignorance (intellectual, moral, political, spiritual, etc.) caused by all kind of factors (poverty, discrimination, lack of pastoral care, etc.) in all kinds of different situations (schools, inner city agencies, RCIA programs, environmental projects, spiritual life centers, etc). But the question giving rise to the particular order is always contextually concrete and can never be answered once and for all or in general. Thus, ministerial innovation by a Religious congregation is not instability or infidelity to its originating charism. Such innovation belongs to the nature of the vocation as prophetic rather than institutional.

It is precisely because the prophet is addressing the actual situation, publicly lamenting current oppression as contrary to God's will, and energizing real people to imagine and begin to strive for an alternate future, that the prophet is often perceived as dangerous to the *status quo*. The "powers that be"—political, economic, religious, ecclesiastical—are powerful precisely because of their position within the current system. They are the agents and beneficiaries of that system. When that system is oppressive the prophet, by encouraging the system's victims toward liberation, is necessarily, and will be perceived by authority as, subversive of the *status quo*.

Furthermore, the prophet is not simply a political organizer or a humanitarian benefactor but is *announcing the Reign of God*, good news to the poor. This good news is not "pie in the sky bye and bye," consolation after death for those who patiently bear irremediable misery in this life. It is "release to captives," "freedom to the oppressed," a new state of affairs, here and now, in which domination, exclusion, stigma, discrimination, oppression of all kinds by state and Church is overcome. The prophet is acting out the universal compassion of God by practicing and empowering people to a practice of justice that will make God's compassion the normal state of affairs, God's reign on earth as it is in heaven.

Finally, the prophet is *sent by God* to proclaim by word and work the coming of the Reign of God in the here and now. The prophet in Israel, including Jesus, was not a priest, elder, rabbi, scribe, Pharisee, or other official. The Religious today, as Religious, is not ordained, not a part of the hierarchical structure of the Church (see *Lumen Gentium* VI, 43, and elsewhere). (Some male Religious are ordained and this creates particular challenges for them that, fortunately, Sisters and Brothers who are simply Religious do not have to deal with and which are beyond the scope of this chapter.) This nonclerical status of Religious has extremely important implications for their prophetic ministry of which many in the Church are unaware or about which they are ill informed.

At ordination the cleric makes a *promise* of obedience *to his ecclesiastical superior*, which binds him *to obey that superior* (and his successors) in relation to the *exercise of his office* in the Church. None of this is true of Religious. Religious make their *vows to God* (not to their superiors or Church officials) *to live Religious Life* (not to exercise some particular function, office, or ministry). Living Religious Life includes the obligations of lifelong profession of the vows. But Religious make their vows *according to* the Constitutions of their order (which includes a particular relationship to Church law), in the *presence of* their superiors, but only *to God*.

In the concrete, this means that Religious, unlike the clergy, are *not agents of the institutional Church* as Jesus was not an agent of institutional Judaism. Although, as members of the Church, they are subject to Church authority when it is legitimately exercised, it is not their "job" or responsibility as Religious to teach, defend, or enforce Church teaching, law, or policy. Because they make public vows Religious are "public persons" in the Church, which means they are bound by canon law in relation to the obligations of their state of life. Religious (like any non-cleric), may exercise a ministry, such as teaching in the RCIA program, which obliges them to correctly represent, in their official ministerial capacity, the teaching and discipline of the magisterium. But this obligation arises from the particular ministry they are exercising, not from their state of life in the Church.

There has been a long history of practical, but theologically and juridically unfounded, assimilation of non-ordained Religious into the hierarchical (or office) structure of the Church. Many Catholics think that that structure includes pope, cardinals, bishops, priests, Religious (in that order), as distinguished from the laity and, therefore, that Religious function as low-level officials or quasi-clerics (without authority or power, of course!) of the institutional Church. Often enough, however, their prophetic vocation leads them, as it led Jesus in his dealing with the woman taken in adultery or with the "unclean" whom he was legally obliged to avoid, to help people deal with situations in their cultural, spiritual, or religious lives for which current law or teaching is inadequate.

Charges of disobedience, unlawful dissent, and so on, are misplaced in such cases. All members of the Church owe respect and accurate representation to official ecclesiastical positions. But not all members of the Church are charged with suppressing thought or dialogue on these subjects (in themselves or others), with enforcing Church law, or with punishing those whose personal situations are more complicated than the law can handle.

Jesus knew and respected the Law and the official teachings of Judaism. Often he even taught them (see, e.g., Mt 5:17, 7:12; Lk 10:25–28, 20:26). But sometimes he gave priority to other equally valid and important considerations such as the suffering of individuals, the inequity of human laws, the fallibility of human interpretation of God's will even on the part of officials. This is an important difference between the ecclesiastical official whose primary duty as an official is to the institution and the prophet whose first duty is facilitating the integration of a concrete situation into the context of the Reign of God. This does not mean that an ecclesiastical official might not be called, at times, to prefer a person to the law or that a prophet might not be called, at times, to vigorously defend an official position. But it does suggest that prophets, in our case Religious, cannot be defined as or reduced to "Temple police." They are not an enforcement agency for the hierarchy's teaching or practice.

This is particularly important in situations that deeply touch the lives of good people trying to live conscientiously and in which the teaching authority of the hierarchy (the magisterium) has not been able to "make its case" to the Church as the People of God. In such cases, there is genuine (even if forbidden and condemned) pluralism of belief and behavior, and even actual valid and legitimate (even if forbidden and condemned) dissent in the Church.

Church teaching, to be considered authoritative, must be not only "promulgated" (announced and adequately explained) but also "received" (accepted by the believing Church). *Humanae Vitae*, for example, promulgated the official position that every act of "artificial" (that is, non-spontaneous) contraception is intrinsically a serious moral evil. Not only did this teaching contradict the conclusions of the papally appointed commission of competent consulters who studied the question in depth, but also neither the clergy who were to teach and enforce this position nor the married people whose lives were intimately affected by this teaching have accepted it. The vast majority of faithful Catholic couples use contraception according to their well-formed consciences to regulate the role of reproduction in their families and most pastoral ministers, ordained or not, make no effort to stop this practice or punish it.

Similar cases of non-reception affect the official teaching concerning the "impossibility" of ordaining women, the "intrinsically disordered" character of homosexuality, the "grave deficiency" of non-Catholic and especially non-Christian religious traditions, the sinfulness of using condoms to prevent the spread of AIDS between spouses, to name only a few "hot button" issues. In these cases the majority of Catholics, including laity, theologians, many pastors, and even some bishops believe that these teachings need revision. In the meantime, ministers, among whom are many Religious, must help people of good will figure out what to do in morally impossible situations.

Insistence that Religious must argue against their own theologically well-grounded judgment, mature experience, and pastoral sensibilities to enforce teachings and policies, which the hierarchy itself cannot defend credibly enough to persuade the majority of the Church's members and cannot actually enforce, is a cooptation of the prophetic ministry of Religious for institutional purposes. It is a cooptation that Religious not only may but must resist.

The widespread, consistent, compassionate ministry of Religious to those suffering from these tensions between the magisterium and the faith convictions of the majority of the People of God often focuses negative hierarchical attention on individual Religious and their congregations as did Jesus' welcoming of sinners and eating with them, breaking purity laws, violating the Sabbath, and releasing the woman taken in adultery. The ministry of Religious to people suffering insoluble conflicts of conscience or caught in impossible life situations is not rebellion or insubordination but a carefully discerned and courageous fidelity to their primary ministerial vocation: to mediate the good news of God's compassion and justice to people in concrete conditions.

Two final implications of the fact that Religious are sent by God and are not, corporately or individually, agents of the institutional Church is that, contrary to what some members of the hierarchy wish were the case, their ministry is not necessarily limited to Catholics or Catholic institutions nor necessarily aimed at sacramental incorporation into the Roman Catholic Church of those to whom they minister. In other words, neither working in Catholic institutions nor conversion of people to Roman Catholicism (which the Council recognized is not identical with the Reign of God) is necessarily the primary vocation of Religious as ministers. The prophetic vocation is to witness by word and work to the Reign of God.

Just as Jesus was deeply rooted in his Jewish identity and community, Religious are deeply rooted in Catholicism as faith tradition and as institutionally organized community. The fundamental "place" of Religious, personally and ministerially, is the Church as the People of God but also as institution with all its sins, scandals, corruption, and violence. Institutional Judaism of the first century was little better, but Jesus never abandoned it, theoretically or practically. And as the ancient prophets and Jesus were sent to Israel to recall it to fidelity to the covenant so that Israel could actually fulfill its vocation to be a "light to the nations," the primary addressee of Religious, corporately and individually, is the Church itself, both its leadership and its members (including themselves as congregations and individuals). However, they are not called as part of the hierarchy to act as agents of the institution but as prophets among the People of God.

Nevertheless, Jesus was drawn beyond his initial understanding of himself as sent "*only* to the lost sheep of the house of Israel" to inclusion in his ministry of pagans (e.g., Mt 15:22–28) and Samaritans (Jn 4:1–42). He did not seem to feel obliged to convert these people to Judaism in order to proclaim the Reign of God to them.

Traditional Catholics over the age of fifty or sixty (to say nothing of many Church officials) might find it hard to imagine "real Sisters" anywhere outside a Catholic institution taking care of Catholics and/or trying to convert non-Catholics. But anyone who has seen the superb traveling museum exhibit "Women and Spirit," which the LCWR has mounted to present the history of women Religious in the United States since they first arrived in the 1700s will be aware that the 1950's type of Religious Life, for which some people nostalgically pine, is actually a relatively recent, short-lived, and somewhat anomalous phenomenon. It parallels the striking, but also anomalous, massive influx of new vocations to Religious Life in the same period. In fact, twentieth-century American women in eighteenth-century European garb moving sedately in pairs from school to nearby convent and back, hands hidden demurely in sleeves or scapular, working quietly under the close supervision of the clergy and relating to "seculars" with quaint Victorian gentility bore very little resemblance to their pioneer forebears.

As women's ministerial Religious Life in the new world gradually emerged from its largely cloistered origins in Europe and scores of new congregations were founded in the new world, the prophetic character of this life was clearly manifest. For the first hundred-plus years at least, the non-cloistered women Religious in this country were most often frontier pioneers ministering in the most diverse and arduous settings imaginable to whoever needed their help.

These Religious lived in log cabins or whatever other shelter was available and wore what they had brought with them or could find or make. They braved the bitter winters of the great plains and the scorching heat of the southwest, cutting their way through woods into rural environments and mountain "hollers." In small groups or alone they criss-crossed the country, over its mountains and across its deserts and up its waterways, by boat, covered wagon, on horseback, by steam engine, and on foot. They nursed on the battlefields, on shipboard, and among the victims of epidemics. They founded schools for native Americans, blacks, and the Appalachian poor and were admitting to their schools and hospitals people of color well before it was legal. They ministered to soldiers and miners and railway workers, to women of "ill repute" and addicts and criminals, and to the orphans whom such populations inevitably leave in their wake. And they rarely discriminated between Catholics and non-Catholics.

In short, their life and ministry was deeply rooted in the Church but not confined to institutions, Catholic or otherwise, nor restricted to their co-religionists, nor aimed in the first instance at conversion. These early American Religious were not an under-developed species awaiting proper institutionalization. They were outstanding exemplars of genuine ministerial Religious Life exercising their prophetic vocation of proclaiming the Reign of God in the unprecedented and challenging frontier context.

When the great wave of immigrants from Catholic countries hit American shores, beginning in the 1820s and increasing steadily through the turn of the century, the Church geared up to serve, and preserve in the faith, these Catholics who were often unwelcome among the established white Protestant and Anglican majority. The Catholic "ghetto," organized around the parish church, depended heavily on women Religious who became, in the eyes of many, the primary representatives of the institutional Church, often outnumbering the local clergy. Women Religious founded and staffed the Catholic institutions that were the primary life-support systems of these early U.S. Catholic communities. In that context, institutions were what was needed for the ongoing proclamation of the Reign of God among the immigrants.

Virtually all Religious were soon living in convents and working in Catholic institutions where they were a kind of service extension of the clergy. The latter defined the "apostolates" of these women and controlled both the work and the Religious themselves, often well beyond the scope of their legitimate authority, which, in any case, was ill-defined. If ever there was a situation of "might makes right," the relation of the clergy to women Religious was it.

This was a period of rapid numerical growth for Religious congregations, which attracted large numbers of the young girls of immigrant families for whom they cared. And as the numbers of recruits increased, large motherhouses and novitiates multiplied as did the institutions in which the Religious ministered.

During this period Religious Life was rapidly institutionalized and domesticated. Though Religious exercised remarkable creativity and zeal in the development, staffing, and administration of the institutions they served, they also became a "standardized" workforce supplying free labor for clerical authorities who suppressed any unapproved initiative of the women and who owned not only most of the institutions in which Sisters served but also the local houses in which they lived and most other resources upon which they depended.

By the early 1900s women's apostolic Religious Life was thoroughly institutionalized and standardized, and, unfortunately, largely domesticated, but also highly successful within a narrow niche which some later labeled, unkindly but not entirely inaccurately, as that of "Father's helpers." This is the image of apostolic Religious familiar from "The Bells of St. Mary's," the idealized and venerated "good Sisters" that many

Catholics remember from their pre-conciliar experience. This type of Religious Life, the hybrid of semi-cloistered monastic life joined to clerically controlled institutionalized apostolic works, was not actually "traditional" or "normative" for ministerial Religious. It was the product of a particular social situation, the ghettoized immigrant Catholic Church in the United States in the mid-1800s to mid-1900s.

The cultural and economic mainstreaming of Catholics, which was well under way by the end of World War II, was officially "accomplished" with the election of John F. Kennedy to the presidency in 1960. With economic and political mainstreaming came the dissolution, for many reasons, of the Catholic parish as religious, social, and cultural ghetto. This sociological revolution, the end of the massive influx of girls from minority ethnic groups into the convent, and the cultural and social tidal waves of the 1960s combined with the renewal of the Second Vatican Council to profoundly change the highly institutionalized Religious Life that had become standard by the first half of the twentieth century. Contemporary ministerial Religious Life, which emerged from this upheaval in the world and the Church, actually looks more like the early ministerial Religious Life of the late seventeenth and eighteenth centuries in Europe and the eighteenth and early nineteenth centuries in the New World!

The Prophetic Life of Contemporary Religious

In this final section I want to discuss the three major changes that the post-conciliar renewal brought about in the living of their prophetic vocation by ministerial Religious and why these changes were and remain so problematic for some conservative Catholics, traditionalist Religious, and the hierarchy. I hope it will become clear why this tension is so often framed in terms of "obedience," as was the objection to the prophetic ministry of Jesus and especially that of his disciples immediately after his execution. This will bring us back to our opening question: what is the deep issue that is at stake in the current investigation of ministerial Religious?

Lifestyle: As a combination of sociological factors in American life and the conciliar developments in the Catholic Church propelled Religious out of the "total institution" lifestyle of the standardization period and into a renewed sense of their vocation to ministry, they made a number of lifestyle changes such as those in regard to habit, housing, and horarium. These developments were important, in fact necessary, for their ministerial life. However, the reaction to them on the part of the hierarchy and traditionalist Catholics (Religious and lay) was completely out of proportion to their theological significance. When the investigation was launched in 2009, however, many people wondered whether the Vatican was trying to "rein in" Religious who had "gone too far" or gotten "out of control." And others, even people not especially familiar with Religious Life, quickly suggested an analogy between the Vatican investigation and the Taliban: that the investigation was simply a patriarchal crack-down on women's autonomy. These observers might have been more astute than even Religious realized!

Religious were certainly not "out of control" but they had, perhaps without particularly attending to it, matured out of *patriarchal* control in highly symbolic ways. The right of religiously empowered males to control women even, and perhaps especially, in the minute and personal details of their lives—what they may (and may not) wear, where and with whom and how they must live, what education and employment is permitted them, to which males they must be accountable, and whose permission is required for any modification of their lives, and so forth is critical to patriarchal control. And in religiously based societies patriarchal control is intrinsic to hierarchical control.

As Religious adjusted their lifestyles to facilitate their expanded involvement in more diversified and individualized ministries, they naturally took the control of such lifestyle issues into their own hands. This had begun back in the 1950s with the Sister Formation Movement when Religious superiors began to make decisions about the education and placement of their Sisters despite hierarchical claims to control of these matters. But it accelerated and touched more, and more visible, aspects of their daily lives in the wake of the Council.

A remarkable number of items on the Phase II questionnaire of the investigation bear upon details of the inner life of congregations and even the personal life of individual Sisters, details that have nothing to do with "quality of life" but have everything to do with minute supervision of every moment and move of the women in question. Why such intrusive examination into the personal life of these women and their communities?

I would suggest that women Religious—being the only part of the female population of the Church to which the male hierarchy has verifiable access and over whom they have the ability to exercise direct coercive power—must be kept under strict and publicly visible control lest the hierarchical power structure itself be called into question. Like Jesus "stirring up the people," women Religious claiming even moderate personal and community autonomy from patriarchal control can seem subversive of hierarchy or at least of the absolute monarchy version of such. The issue, once again, is cast in terms of "obedience." But the real issue is power. Even if nothing else in Religious Life had changed, these developments in regard to lifestyle could well have precipitated the panic-reaction that launched the investigation.

Community: However there *was* something else, and at a deeper level. The stabilization period (mid-nineteenth to mid-twentieth century) gave rise to a (mis)understanding of women's Religious Life that most Religious themselves and Church officials generally shared, namely, that Religious Life was structurally modeled on the hierarchical Church, which was understood and functioned as a pyramidal divine-right monarchy.

Of course, the superior at the pinnacle of the Religious congregation's pyramid, even though elected by the members, actually received even her "ordinary" (i.e., office) authority by delegation from the ordained and operated always in dependence on and by permission of that authority. In that respect she differed from her analogues in the ecclesiastical hierarchy who held their ordinary authority by virtue of ordination. But, otherwise, the congregation with general superior, provincials, local superiors, and powerless "subjects" mirrored the hierarchical Church with pope, bishops, priests, and powerless "laity." Each level's incumbents were, ideally, obedient (even blindly so) to those of the level above. There was little or no distinction between authority and coercive power.

Under the influence of the Gospel-based conciliar ecclesiology of the People of God combined with the theologically and culturally enlightened rethinking of Religious Life by Sisters themselves from the 1950s into the late 1960s, women Religious simply stepped—sideways as it were—out of the pyramidal structure that had controlled their lives up to that point. They affirmed the fundamental equality of all members in a class- and caste-free community, opted for collegial government, and affirmed the profession-based rather than political character of their life together.

Obedience ceased to be understood as blind submission to divinely empowered, absolute, and non-accountable official "authorities." Rather, corporate obedience meant the full and free cooperation of all members of the community with congregational leaders and each other in co-responsibility for their life and mission. Individual obedience was an exercise in mutual discernment between the Religious and her congregation's leadership.

Although Religious themselves, in general, made this transition from divine-right monarchy to a discipleship of equals with relative speed, though not without strenuous effort and much suffering—perhaps because the new form was far more compatible with women's ways of doing things than were the quasi-military, autocratic procedures they had inherited from male authority—the institutional Church's official leadership has never been comfortable with this development. The Vatican has struggled for decades against the egalitarianism, collegiality, team leadership models, binding consultation of members, dialogical procedures, discernment processes, practice of subsidiarity, and commitment to non-violent conflict resolution and a non-coercive exercise of authority that women Religious have adopted.

Religious have respectfully but firmly resisted Vatican attempts to restore sacralized autocracy in their lives and communities. Blind obedience, within their congregations or to Church officials, is no longer considered a virtue by these Religious and very few, if any, congregational leaders in renewed communities would think seriously of trying to demand it. Religious know that "blind obedience" is not only theologically highly suspect (not just for Religious but for any Christian) but that it does not work nearly as well as the communitarian form of government that has replaced it.

Religious, both by the contemplative prayer that grounds their life and by their free choice of and deepened appropriation of consecrated celibacy, evangelical poverty, and prophetic obedience, have reconstructed their lives to maximize their freedom from the kinds of influences and pressures—from persons, possessions, and power (civil and ecclesiastical)—that would tempt them to ignore or distort the voices that they are actually hearing, or prevent their seeing "the signs of the times" pointing to God's will in the present situation. Their way of living in community is highly conducive to the ministerial exercise of their prophetic vocation of focusing the word of God in the concrete situations in which they minister. (For an engrossing account of one congregation's amazing, but very typical, journey through this transformation, see Phyllis Kittel's fascinating oral history-based account, *Staying in the Fire*, 2009).

In effect, Religious—probably without consciously intending such a thing—were subverting the domination system of the patriarchal Church by incarnating in their community life an alternative not only to patriarchy but to all forms of coercion-based exercise of power. This is a more serious challenge to an absolutist hierarchy than the challenge to its patriarchal control of women members because it is based in and incarnates an ecclesiology of equal discipleship in which no one is called rabbi or teacher or father because there is only one teacher, Christ, and one Parent, God, and all members of the community are sisters and brothers (see Mt 23:8–11).

Ministry: Both lifestyle changes, which challenged patriarchy and the development of collegial community life that incarnated *Lumen Gentium*, the conciliar ecclesiology of the Church as the People of God, made hierarchical authority very uneasy. However, both these developments were internal to Religious Life itself. Both raised the issue of obedience, the first of women to men and the second of laity to ordained. But as women Religious moved out of the collective institutional ministries in Catholic settings (schools, etc.) in which they had functioned for many decades and into highly diversified and individualized ministries in fields inside and outside the institutional Church setting, they unleashed a third unsettling force with which the hierarchy had to deal, namely, prophetic ministry. In this arena the issue of obedience became paramount.

Religious were now involved in the precarious business of trying to proclaim the Reign of God in concrete situations in which Church teaching, law, and policy often were not easy to communicate to people who were trying to form their consciences, make good moral decisions, choose the best option among a range of bad possibilities, or just stay alive when nothing was working for them. Teaching catechism to ten-year-olds in 1950 and helping a woman with five small children decide what to do about a virtually certainly fatal pregnancy were simply not in the same category. Sisters were now ministering in prisons, with undocumented immigrants, in inner-city shelters, on Capitol Hill, in spirituality centers open to all faiths or none, with the homeless, with torture victims, with the dying who were alienated from the Church, and in myriad other situations in which there were no easy answers, and the stakes for real people were as high as they were for the woman taken in adultery to whom Jesus proclaimed the Reign of God as compassion redefining justice.

The theological issue at the heart of this situation was that raised by *Gaudium et Spes*, namely, how does the Church of Jesus Christ understand and relate to the world? Is the Church a fortress of truth and moral righteousness in a sea of wickedness, charged with protecting her own from contamination while naming and condemning the evil of the surrounding culture—an approach those over sixty will remember well? Or is the Church the suffering Body of Christ in solidarity with all that is human as real people, individually and as a race, struggle toward the light of the Resurrection? The ministerial choices of Religious in the aftermath of the Council were increasingly an affirmation of the latter. But this often placed prophetic ministers in tension with Church authority. The tension tended to be framed as a conundrum of obedience.

In a sense, the topic can be adumbrated by re-reading the episode in the Acts of the Apostles 5:19–42 in which Peter and his companions preach the Gospel of Jesus as the Christ and his inauguration of the Reign of God after being forbidden by the Temple hierarchy to do so:

> The high priest questioned them, saying, "We gave you strict orders not to teach in this name, yet here you have filled Jerusalem with your teaching and you are determined to bring this man's blood on us." But Peter and the apostles answered, "We must obey God rather than any human authority." (Acts 5:27–30)

All the elements of the conflict situation are here: the hierarchical order not to preach the Gospel because that preaching constituted a threat to the institutional *status quo* and its authorities and the disciples' response contrasting human (including hierarchical) authority with divine authority.

The disciples defended themselves not by claiming that the high priest had no authority but simply by saying that, in a case of conflict between what God had charged them to do in service of the Word and what even legitimate religious authority commanded them to do, they followed their consciences. They were flogged and again commanded to cease bearing witness to the paschal mystery. But they rejoiced to suffer for fulfilling their vocation and continued boldly to preach the word in private and in public as Jesus had charged them and the Holy Spirit had empowered them to do. Hierarchical authority in the Church, as in the Sanhedrin, is real and legitimate but it is not absolute. As Paul said, there are many charisms in the Church and none of them simply usurps or controls all the others (see 1 Cor 12).

In the scene just evoked, Gamaliel, a Pharisee, addressed his fellows in the Sanhedrin with timelessly valid advice:

> So in the present case, I tell you, keep away from
> these men [the disciples] and let them alone; be-
> cause if this plan or this undertaking [their preach-
> ing of the Gospel] is of human origin, it will fail; but
> if it is of God, you will not be able to overthrow
> them—in that case you may even be found fighting
> against God! (Acts 5:38-39)

The current conflicts between hierarchical authority and the exercise of their prophetic ministry by women Religious has been escalating since the institutional renewal of Religious Life began in the early 1970s. Implicit in the call of the Vatican Council to Religious to renew their lives for the sake of ministry in and to the world which the Council itself had embraced in a new way is a new understanding of their practice of obedience as rooted in the prophetic nature of Religious Life itself. Religious began to embrace a call to ministry fully compatible with their vocation, indeed more compatible in many ways than the standardized institutional apostolates of the past century. They began to reclaim the specifically ministerial (but non-ordained) nature of their life which was, in effect, a reclaiming of its prophetic character.

This ministerial renewal has been, in many respects, more unsettling for the institutional authorities than the internal lifestyle and community renewal was, but for the same reasons. Religious were no longer as easily controllable by the clergy. They could no longer be "ordered up" as troops for institutional campaigns and "deployed where needed" by the hierarchy. Where once there had been twenty Religious staffing one institution under the control of the local clergy, now there were one or two, ministering in many initiatives, sometimes beyond the borders of Catholic institutions, and empowering in ministry groups of laity newly conscious of their own call to ministry.

Ecclesiastical authority, at least in the reigns of the last two popes, often has been an exercise in the suppression of all voices except its own, branding as "dissent" (always understood as sinful disobedience rather than mature critical engagement) any position, and sometimes even the consideration of arguments for any position, at variance with "official teaching." Religious obedience, however, is precisely an exercise of a prophetic vocation calling its members to carefully discern the meaning of the Word of God in and for a particular situation.

Here we see very clearly the point of tension, namely, *two different understandings of obedience.* The hierarchical definition of obedience is total, blind, and absolute submission in thought, word, and deed, interiorly and exteriorly, to office authority. Any deviation from this understanding constitutes dissent, which is always sinful, and if acted upon, is disobedience. The prophetic definition of obedience is the prayerful listening for the will of God in all relevant "voices" and the search for that will in the "signs of the times," followed by careful discernment and responsible speaking and acting out of that discernment for the good of real people in concrete situations. This may at times involve dissent, not as defiance or disobedience but as creative contribution to a fuller discernment of and obedience to the will of God in the present situation.

Obedience, in other words is not about mindless submission; it is an explicit commitment to mindful discernment. If God's will coincided exactly, always, and exhaustively with the teaching or legislating of office holders, no discernment, of course, would be necessary or legitimate. But the example of Jesus makes it abundantly clear that this is not the case and no one is dispensed from the challenge of discernment, even when the teaching or law in question is derived from scripture itself.

This has led to the kinds of tensions discussed above in which Religious are no longer simply "channeling" official teaching or enforcing Church policy but ministering to people in concrete situations of suffering and struggle and having to help those people discern what God is doing in their lives and calling them to, which often enough cannot be fully identified with official teaching or policy.

Many lay people of all ages and conditions have emerged in the past few months bearing witness to the role women Religious have played in sustaining their faith and often their Church affiliation through experiences of rejection, denial of the sacraments or Christian burial for their family members, excommunication, and public shaming at the hands of hierarchical authority defending and enforcing its teaching, which it equated with God's will. The outreach of Religious to the socially marginalized and ecclesiastically alienated is not a matter of contradicting authority, any more than was Jesus' approach to the authorities who had arrested the woman taken in adultery. It is a matter of compassion, offered in the name of the God of the prodigal (who we all are), to suffering sisters and brothers of Jesus without conditioning that compassion on moral rectitude or theological orthodoxy. It is possible to say both "You are accepted and loved, unconditionally, just as you are" and, when a person is strong enough to hear it, "Sin no more."

For the past four decades Religious have been living into a new understanding of Religious Life itself involving a new understanding of their ministry as prophetic. This, in turn, has involved a new understanding of obedience. They have been living into the vision inaugurated by the Second Vatican Council of the Church as the People of God who are the ministerial Body of Christ in this world. And as they have lived into this reality themselves, Religious have been, for many, the most convincing corporate witness in the Church to the truth and power of the conciliar vision of Christian identity and vocation. They have been calling the laity and even some of the clergy to be Church in a new way, and modeling the possibility of that kind of Christian faith and life. However, beginning seriously with the pontificate of John Paul II, the hierarchical Church began a retrenchment from Vatican II, which has become increasingly a Tridentine restorationism under the current pope. These two visions of Church, that of the Council and that of the restoration, are running, one forward and one backward, on parallel ecclesiological tracks.

CONCLUSION

We can now see the parallel between the two-level analysis of the execution of Jesus and the two levels of the struggle between U.S. women Religious and the Vatican. At the surface level Jesus was executed to put a stop to his "stirring up the people," which threatened the *status quo* of the Empire and the Temple. But at the deepest level, although "they knew not what they were doing," the officials were trying to neutralize the radical revolution Jesus was introducing into their well-ordered and controlled "world." Jesus was initiating, by his prophetic words and works, a "new creation," totally at odds with the satanic domination systems in power not only in political and religious institutions but in the human race as a whole. He was inaugurating and inviting people into the Reign of God, into a regime of endless and unconditional compassion that would overflow into and empower a new form of justice based not on retribution and coercive power but on forgiveness of sins and inclusion in the all-embracing love of God. The Resurrection was God's "yes" to Jesus' work and "no" to the murder that tried to stop it.

Since Jesus, the Reign of God is "loose" in this world, working its painful way through the witness of saints and martyrs toward its full eschatological realization. The "powers" of this world are still at work to prevent this realization but, as Jesus said to his disciples on the eve of his death, "Have confidence; I have overcome the world" (Jn 16:33).

When we get down to the deeper levels of the question with which this chapter began, "Why are Religious, of all people, being investigated by the Vatican?" we can discern the same two levels. At the surface level Religious are being threatened because they have been "upsetting the (patriarchal) order" of the Church as institution in which the hierarchy has its position of power. But they are calling into question not only absolute male power over women (which was not invented by and is not restricted to the Church) but also the understanding of the Church itself as essentially an institution based on sacralized power, a divine-right monarchy. Religious, by their community life, are aligning themselves with the ecclesiology of the Church as People of God expressed in *Lumen Gentium,* a discipleship of equals, within which they are both exemplars and facilitators but also in solidarity with those to whom they no longer wish to be "superior" or "elite." They are gratefully living, among their lay sisters and brothers, the oneness of the Body of Christ. This ecclesiology is no threat to the community Jesus gathered around him but it is a threat to an understanding of Church as a sacralized empire. The community called Church goes back to Jesus, not to Constantine.

But this Body of Christ, which we are, exists not just for the Church itself but for the world which God so loved. It is not a place of privilege or power, a sanctuary of the perfect, but the effective presence of Christ in the world in service of all those for whom Jesus died and rose. This is the vision of the Church in the world that came to marvelous expression at the Council in *Gaudium et Spes.*

The struggle between Religious and the hierarchy is really, at its core, a struggle over the nature of Religious Life itself, which is necessarily determined by how one understands the Church in its relation to the world. Is this life a job corps of submissive workers carrying out hierarchically assigned and supervised institutional Church tasks designed to bring all people into the Roman Catholic Church and into subjection to its leadership? Or is Religious Life a charismatically grounded, prophetic lifeform in the Church called by God to the ever ambiguous task of discerning how the Gospel, the good news of the Reign of God, can be made salvifically operative in the concrete and confusing situations in which believers must live their Christ-life today in witness to all peoples of the infinite loving-kindness of our God?

If, as I believe, it is the latter, then the primary "offense" of ministerial Religious is that they are reading the "signs of the times" as a call to sustain and promote the renewal inaugurated by Vatican II while some officials of the institution itself are trying to restore the Tridentine vision of the Church as a power structure defending itself against a threatening world that is promoting a culture of death. Like the disciples preaching Jesus as the crucified messiah when they had been told by the authorities that that interpretation of the paschal events was false, threatening to the authorities, and not to be proclaimed, Religious are embodying in their lives and proclaiming to others an interpretation of the Council that is not approved by many in the hierarchy. Rather than "obediently" supporting the restoration, they are promoting the ongoing conciliar renewal in their own lives and among the laity.

The re-centralization of power in the Vatican, the re-clericalization of ministry, the restoration of liturgy as a mysterious and private clerical performance to which the baptized are an appreciative but passive audience, and the reduction of spirituality to private devotionalism—all of which are central to the restorationist agenda—are endangered by the theology of Vatican II, which Religious are living and promoting. Gamaliel's test is the only one that will eventually adjudicate this difference of interpretation. Was the Council a definitive and irreversible Pentecostal renewal of the Church, which, no matter how difficult it will be to do so, must be lived into the future, and, in any case, cannot be suppressed any more than the apostolic preaching could be? Or was it the mistake of false "enthusiasts" that needs to be corrected by a "reform of the reform"? That adjudication is going to take considerable time.

It is difficult to see how the ongoing tension between official authority and Religious Life that is part of this Church-wide struggle can be resolved. But a first step toward non-violence and mutuality, even in difference, is to recognize the problem. Religious, it seems to me, need to claim and define their own life as they have come to understand it and live it with courage and integrity but without arrogance or unnecessary provocation. Religious Life is not a grade on the hierarchical ladder; it does not belong to the hierarchical structure of the Church at all. It is a charismatically grounded close following and imitation of Jesus and his itinerant band of disciples. The vocation to prophetic ministry is intrinsic to this lifeform. This is true of the lifeform itself and therefore of congregations and individual members.

Most Religious I know deeply desire open communication, understanding, mutual respect, and cooperation in ministry within the institutional Church. They have consistently shown themselves willing to go much more than the "extra mile" to achieve this goal. But they are not willing to de-nature their life or ministry any more than the first disciples were willing to "not preach in that name any more" when ordered to cease.

A second step, at least so it seems to me, is for Religious to pray their way, personally and corporately, into a peaceful and courageous acceptance that the tension between institutional authority and prophetic ministry is and will always be part of the life of the Body of Christ, the journey of

the People of God through history, because it was structurally intrinsic to Jesus' own prophetic life and ministry.
Part of understanding Religious Life today, for Religious
themselves and for others, is a double realization. First,
prophetic ministry is absolutely necessary for the Church in
every age, even though it probably will never be welcomed
by institutional authority. Second, the exercise of that ministry, which is intrinsic to Religious Life, will always involve
misunderstanding of one's best intentions, persecution and
suffering, and sometimes even crucifixion, which Jesus told
his disciples at the last supper, often may be at the hands of
the religious authorities who think that thereby "they are
giving glory to God" (Jn 16:2).

Religious cannot expect to experience Jesus' resurrection
if we are unwilling to share his passion. And we do not always
have the luxury of choosing whether we will suffer at the
hands of secular powers or of the Church's power structure.
But Jesus says to us as he did to Paul in the midst of his ministerial struggles, which came most often from the religious
rather than the secular authorities, "My grace is sufficient for
you, for power is made perfect in weakness" (2 Cor 12:9).

CONCLUSION

Religious Life in the Wake of the Investigations

Anyone who has ministered to people who are suffering has probably encountered the anguished question, "Why did God...": give this young mother terminal cancer? allow our child to be kidnapped and killed? inflict this hurricane upon an already earthquake-ravaged country? Conversely, there are those smug or masochistic or sadistic people who are sure they know exactly why "God did" something: God is punishing those perverts, God is testing my faith, God took your child to teach you detachment, and so on. This attribution of direct causality for intra-mundane happenings to God can be a spontaneous reaction to bewilderment in the face of inexplicable evil and suffering but it reflects bad theology and encourages worse spirituality. Before looking for traces of God's influence in the present experience of the Vatican investigations of Religious congregations and their leadership, it is well to unveil and repudiate any temptation to whitewash that experience under the rubric of "God's will."

The conviction that God governs the universe by direct miraculous interventions in everything from keeping the rain from ruining our picnic to permitting epidemics that decimate whole populations allows us to believe that "Someone" is in charge and therefore to blame (or to be thanked) for every happening, large or small. It convinces us that we are not really alone in a chance-driven universe. However capricious, cruel, inscrutable, or violent we have to believe this "Universe Controller" to be, at least we do not have to face the terror that there is no all-powerful Hand on the cosmic tiller.

But eventually, if we are to mature spiritually, we have to surrender this magical approach to reality, this need for "Someone" who can be held responsible for what we cannot fathom or control, whom we can blame or cower before or bribe or cajole in the face of life's uncertainties. We have to face the fact that germs, atmospheric conditions, the movement of tectonic plates, human malice or stupidity (our own or someone else's), just being in the wrong place at the wrong time, or myriad other factors which we do not even know about and which God is not manipulating by some giant computer in the sky—in other words, cause and effect in the finite space-time continuum in which we live—accounts for "what happens" that is outside our knowledge or control or that is contrary to our will.

God is always present to us, more intimate to us than we are to ourselves, deeply and lovingly concerned about us down to the very hairs on our head (see Mt 10:30). God is supporting us, urging us to the best responses to reality of which we are capable and even beyond what we think we are capable of, consoling us in suffering, sharing and affirming our joy, strengthening us in conflict, and enabling us to learn and grow through everything we experience no matter how tragic or overwhelming it may be. But this does not make God the direct and immediate efficient cause of each event that happens in the universe.

This is what we learn from the crucifixion of Jesus. God did not will the unmitigated evil of the murder of Jesus, much less kill him for our sakes. Jesus' murderers were not God's secret co-workers or disguised instruments of the divine will, and deicide is not the cause of our salvation. But God was with Jesus right through death itself and, by raising

Jesus from the dead, set the seal of divine approval on Jesus' free choice to give life to us, even at the cost of his own. This central event of Christian experience, God's drawing the salvation of the world from Jesus' willing acceptance of the absolute evil wreaked upon him by demonically inspired human hatred, is the pattern of what we call the "paschal mystery," the victorious emergence of life from the very bowels of death. Death does not cause life, but life triumphs even over death because life is of God. In short, bad causes, whether natural disasters or accidents or stupidity or human evil, do not produce good results, but human beings dealing courageously and creatively with natural or moral evil can cause great good to emerge for themselves and others.

Christians down through the ages have shared in this paschal mystery, in large and small ways, following in the footsteps of the crucified and risen Jesus. How often we have heard people say, "I'd give anything in the world not to have done what I did...not to have suffered this loss...not to have been the victim of...—but I would not have become the person I am today if that tragedy had not entered my life." Christianity is not a masochistic glorification of victimhood, much less a sadistic divine infliction of suffering "to build character." It is not the case, for example, that the domestic abuse of this woman was a good thing because it "enabled" her to take charge of her life. *She*, her courage and determination, God's grace, perhaps the help of others and resources available at the right time and place, *not her being abused*, is what enabled her to rise out of a hell of evil and choose life. And the lack of those resources might make another woman unable to escape the evil but still able to keep her integrity in the midst of it. And a third might simply succumb to the evil. In no case does faith make evil good. But faith can make suffering meaningful, struggle worthwhile, victory affirming, and even the acceptance of what we cannot surmount life giving, as they were for Jesus.

Many people, in and outside Religious Life, are beginning to realize that two Vatican investigations of U.S. women Religious and their leaders, which have caused enormous expenditures of material and human resources, sidetracking of valuable time and energy of congregations and their leaders, distraction from ministry and community life, while generating widespread anxiety especially among Religious living the final days of decades-long lives of fidelity and dedication to God's people, have nevertheless been the context for some very positive developments. These developments were clearly not intended by the investigations and certainly not caused by them. But God is not limited by human intentions and, like the woman who takes charge of her life in a way she would not have had she been in an even minimally tolerable marriage, Religious well beyond the limits of the targeted object of the investigations—namely, U.S. women Religious—are taking hold consciously of their Council-inspired identity and mission in a powerful new way. It can be life giving to pay attention to some of these developments even as we clearly recognize and affirm them as the work of the Spirit strengthening our spirits to endure suffering and grow through it, not as the product of human intimidation.

Perhaps the most important development is the impetus given by the suspicion cast on American Religious Life by the very launching of the investigations to articulate much more clearly the theology and spirituality that has developed within and energized the last forty years of ministerial Religious Life in this country. Religious during these decades were busy living their way into a new stage in the history of their life and sharing their life with the people to whom they ministered. But the calling into question of the integrity of their personal and communal lives, the fidelity of their commitment to Church and Religious Life, and the efficacy of the renewal they undertook in response to the Council's invitation and mandate, has stimulated an overdue effort to speak their truth clearly to themselves and in the assembly of the People of God.

A second development is that this self-articulation has resonated deeply with the actual experience of women Religious in and by the U.S. Church and this has elicited a spirited expression of appreciation and support of the Sisters by many thousands of lay Catholics and some of the clergy. Not only are Sisters not seen as lax, unfaithful, in need of investigation of the "quality of their life" and correction (or perhaps even suppression) by a hierarchy that could be better employed examining its own affairs, but they are widely perceived as sources of inspiration and support by millions of Catholics who themselves have been trying to internalize the teaching of Vatican II and to live its spirit in their families, parishes, and professional settings. As the laity has sprung to the support of the Sisters, the Sisters have realized in a new way how intimately connected their life has become to that of their lay sisters and brothers. Both groups have affirmed and rejoiced in their life-giving solidarity, especially in a scandal-ridden Church whose institutional integrity is in shambles and whose public agenda is increasingly restorationist.

A third paschal development has been the recognition by Religious of the deep unity among themselves, across congregational lines, that has developed in the wake of the Council. If there was a time in the past when Religious thought of themselves first as members of their own congregations, not only distinct from but even in competition with other congregations, that time is long past. For decades Religious have been ministering together, sharing resources and facilities, looking to each other for support and affirmation, which often was not forthcoming from ecclesiastical authorities. But that solidarity has come to new expression in the past two years as all Religious have found themselves together under a cloud of implied censure. The stunning courage of the LCWR, already under investigation and therefore with good reason to think first of its own safety, in supporting the effort to pass health care reform legislation for millions of unprotected Americans—a support that was echoed by the vast majority of women Religious—was a remarkable expression of unified leadership and cross-congregational solidarity in ministry. At this point Religious tend to see themselves first as Religious and then as Sisters of St. Joseph or the Immaculate Heart of Mary. We now know that there are sixty thousand of us, and that is a formidable cohort for speaking truth to power and promoting justice for the voiceless.

An amazing development that can only be the work of the Spirit has been the emergence into voice of Religious throughout the world—especially in the two-thirds world—expressing their support for and solidarity with their U.S. Sisters under siege. The statement of support of the International Union of Superiors General (UISG) and of the Religious of Asia and Oceania (AMOR) as well as of other groups of Religious who all have risked "guilt by association" for their loyalty to their American Sisters has been humbling and exhilarating for U.S. Religious, used perhaps to a leadership role among Religious but less used to being the beneficiaries of the support and care of Religious from other parts of the world. As I have traveled nationally and internationally over the past two years I have been surprised—and yet not surprised—at the concern for, the solidarity with, the support of Religious all over the world in regard to American Religious. We are not merely sixty thousand strong but many times that. And the vast majority of us are very much on the same page in our response to the challenges of the Council to be a new Church in and for and with the world that God so loves.

There are other developments emerging, not as clear or unambiguous, but worth watching. Have we been underestimating the immense vitality of that cohort of vigorous women who are being studied increasingly by sociologists as the subjects of a new developmental life stage that has enormous potential for world culture, the so-called "third-agers"? These people, who will soon be the largest and fastest growing age cohort in the world, are healthy, active, and engaged people who are between sixty-five and eighty-five or older, which is precisely where the bulk of women Religious are today.

Are we taking time to interact with younger women who, as they were growing up, may not have known personally any Sisters and perhaps thought of them as timid and domesticated "good little nuns" or "father's little helpers" but who now are hearing and reading about educated and powerful women Religious committed to a Vatican II Church and a redeemed world? Are we inviting them to think about women living community as equal adults, who are deeply Catholic but not institutional functionaries, who are fully involved in both the single-hearted quest for God and full-time commitment to the development of a new world of peace and justice, and who are not owned by, or cowed by, or beholden to male power? Do we have something to offer to our younger sisters that we have not articulated with sufficient clarity but that we are responsible to pass on to new generations?

Adversity often calls out of people conviction, strength, and commitment that they were not conscious of possessing. That does not make adversity, especially gratuitous adversity caused by human beings, a blessing, even a "blessing in disguise." It may well take considerable time, even after these investigations are a vague and distant memory, to fully realize what we have learned from this experience. At the very least it should make us newly aware that Religious Life is indeed, as the Council called it, a gift—to the Church itself, to those called to it, to those in other states of life in the Church, to those to whom Religious minister—and that such a gift should not be taken for granted.